AF333733

In a Family Way

In a Family Way

*A Husband and Wife's Diary of Pregnancy,
Birth and the First Year of Parenthood*

SUSAN LAPINSKI AND
MICHAEL DE COURCY HINDS

Little, Brown and Company   Boston   Toronto

FIRST EDITION

The authors are grateful to the following publishers for permission to quote material noted below:

Children's Press for excerpts from WHEELS OF THE BUS GO ROUND AND ROUND by Nancy Larrick Crosby. Reprinted with permission.

Ginn and Company for "The Kind Kangaroo" from *Tuning Up* of THE WORLD OF MUSIC series, © copyright 1943, 1936, by Ginn and Company (Xerox Corporation). Used with permission.

Library of Congress Cataloging in Publication Data

Lapinski, Susan.
  In a family way.

  1. Lapinski, Susan. 2. Hinds, Michael
deCourcy. 3. Parents — Biography. 4. Childbirth.
5. Infants. 6. Family. I. Hinds, Michael
deCourcy. II. Title.
HQ755.8.L36A34 1982 306.8'7'0922 82-12681
ISBN 0-316-51444-6

BP

Designed by Janis Capone

*Published simultaneously in Canada
by Little, Brown & Company (Canada) Limited*

Printed in the United States of America

For Jessica

"Are you writing this down?" Michael would prod me, the family diary-keeper, every time we reached a milestone en route to becoming parents. Before long, he stopped relying on me and started taking his own notes. We both wanted a record of our progress as a family for ourselves and, someday, for Jessica.

Michael wrote on anything handy, I wrote in a red-silk-covered journal when I had time, and on an appointment calendar when I didn't. In any form, our diaries helped us to capture events and feelings that might otherwise have floated away in a flood of everyday details.

Shortly before Jessica's first birthday, a magazine editor asked us to prepare a portion of the diaries for publication. For the first time, we shuffled our entries together chronologically, and began reading each other's.

On the way to this book, we have amplified some cryptic entries, dropped some repetitious ones, and left in others so personal that we still have second thoughts about including them. But mostly the diary stands as it was written. Like Jessica, it is a labor of love.

In a Family Way

February 23
Somewhere on the high seas between Jamaica and Aruba, Michael and I realized that we want to have a baby. No, it's not a new idea for us. We've thought of it, off and on, through five married years — while we've both worked at our writing, traveled in Europe, moved from Boston to New York. But somehow, being on a Caribbean cruise has slowed us down and smoothed us out enough to consider the next chapter.

Maybe it's because we've been twisting hips to steel drums in the moonlight. Or because our cabin steward takes creative liberties with my silk pajamas when he arranges them on my pillow. Or because a friendly older couple from Chicago, who have four beautiful daughters, whispered to us over rum drinks tonight, "You really ought to have a child."

Actually, it's none of these. The fact is, I've always known that I wanted to have a baby. I melt at the sight of a toothless pink smile, a lace bonnet on a downy head. Michael invariably smirks at my enthusiasm and calls all children "midgets," but I've noticed he's wonderful with friends' kids, toting them on his shoulders, tumbling around with them like a puppy.

In the past, whenever people have asked if we wanted children, I've carefully replied that we could be happy with them or without them. But now I sometimes ache at the thought of never making a child of our own.

Michael / Aboard the Federico "C"

February 23
The "Ship's News," a ten-paragraph link to the outside world, provides an unwelcome pinch of reality as we drift through paradise, leisurely taking notes and photographs for the story we were sent here to work on. Today, the news is that the Mideast is in its usual chaos, Russia and China are shaking missiles at one another, and three billion cubic feet of snow is falling on New York City.

The only snow we've seen on the *Federico "C"* is the ice under our Beluga caviar. The international disputes here involve decisions to dance under the stars to Barbadian rhythms or to disco belowdecks, to swim in the Italian pool or to venture into the Latin American ports that flutter past like a sheaf of postcards.

At least once a day someone asks if Susie and I are honeymooning. At first, we said no, but have since decided yes is the right answer. Anyway, the old-timers are put off balance when they hear we've been married five years. We don't have that settled-down look, and I guess that's unsettling.

A nice thing about paradise, aside from cappuccino in silver pots, is the endless time to gaze up at one's thoughts and see them from new angles. The most startling new angle: we both think we're ready to have a baby. What an exciting, terrifying idea.

Susan / Aboard the Federico "C"

February 24
I'm on deck, in a low-slung chair. Rosario, who is one of the sailors and an Ernest Borgnine look-alike, just brewed

himself some espresso, and brought me a cup, too. With the coffee come stories of his family, at home in Sicily. His stubby hands spin visions of a house by the sea, children with ripe-olive eyes, a wife who hangs pasta to dry in the sun.

Rosario's stories are a perfect fit for my mood. I'm feeling nostalgic about family, crazy for a baby. The boat's rocking motion seems to have gone right to my head.

If I really dared to think about it, I'm sure I'd have more second thoughts. On most easygoing days with Michael, I feel like a child myself, still playing house after all these years. I know so little about babies. And, living in a New York City shoebox, we hardly have the space for one.

But with the equatorial sun softening the brain, and my thirty-year-old hormones going haywire, who can think?

Michael / Aboard the **Federico "C"**

February 24

"Did you see that beautiful baby, Michael?" Susie always asks, as every wrinkled, drooling creature passes by. I respond, ritually, "You say that about every baby."

The decision to have a baby was not a decision. It was an emotion. Do I trust the emotion to have a child? I don't think so. On that confident note, let's once, and possibly for all time, review the pros and cons of having a baby.

The cons, which are easiest to spin off:
- Loss of freedom. To pick up and go dancing, traveling.
- Loss of our couple's relationship. Our long date might come to an end.

- The pathetic world. Should we really bring a new person onto this war-threatened, polluted planet?
- The defect question. If the baby is born retarded, disabled. How will we and s/he feel about it? Regretful? Resentful?
- Screaming kids. A lot of work and tension seem to be involved in this endeavor. Overheard stories of parents not being able to sleep at night or past dawn. Tantrums and discipline.
- Space. In a small New York apartment, where do you store the children? When I see people walking Saint Bernards, Great Danes or children, I always wonder how they manage it.
- Loss of cash. Kids are expensive. Neighbor said it was going to cost him fifty thousand dollars to put his child through private schools, another forty thousand dollars through college, not counting inflation. Or baby-sitters, braces, bubble gum and summer camp.
- The uncertainties. Who are children and what do they want? Could I do a good job as a father? Am I too moody?

The pros, which require more effort to think up:

- A baby would make Susie happy, perhaps ecstatic.
- A baby might center our lives. I have a feeling that we are going off course. New York, careers and trivia take precedence over the things we truly value. We have less time for each other. A baby might domesticate us, bring us back in touch with the simple, most rewarding pleasures.
- I do like children.
- People with children seem pleased with their lot. Seemingly, to an insane degree. At work, Mother Jane is always heaping praise on her dwarfs. Says I've "got" to have them, too.

Add it up, and what do I get? Nothing new, no easy conclusion. It's something you can't calculate, I guess. The time may never be right. It all boils down to "I want" or "I don't want." Susie wants. I want to want. Therefore, we will! Lord be merciful.

Susan / Miami, Florida

February 25
As I walked down the gangplank today, I felt a slow, sunny world fall away beneath my feet. At the end of the runway were all the hard facts our cruise left behind: a new job to break in, our need for a bigger apartment, the changes our baby decision will surely bring.

While the steel bands tinkled and the champagne flowed, the distant prospect of a baby lulled us both. Now that the cruise is over, having a child seems like a revolutionary idea that could threaten other things Michael and I want: time to write, to travel, to be together.

Reality has hit me in the face like this muggy day in Miami.

Michael / New York

March 15
The more we talk about babies, the more real they seem. And the more real the problems seem. Take Susie's view of abortion: she will never have one, even if tests show the baby would have birth defects. This is a difficult attitude to understand.

She has always believed in other women's right to make the choice, and I guess I just assumed that meant she would also have an abortion under the appropriate circumstances.

So last night I was floored when she said it would be pointless to take the amniocentesis test after getting pregnant. Negative test results would only be upsetting, she said, since her conscience would not allow her to stop the pregnancy.

Naturally, I tried to dissuade her from this Catholic thought. I used the old arguments that it is more charitable to abort a fetus than to insist that a brain-damaged child struggle through life. But to her, these are imponderables. She could not do it.

I see her point but it scares me. I don't know if I'm tough enough to handle a normal little bruiser, never mind a disabled one who requires constant attention for life.

I'm getting to know this woman, my wife.

Michael

April 18

Anybody who calls you "Spike" has got to be a good friend. That's Charles Paul. He calls Susie "Spikette." In revenge, I call him "Chucka," but, as yet, I have not stooped to nicknaming Suzanne, his magnificent wife, "Chuckette."

Charles and Suzanne came to visit. I was eager to see them because they are a family. Since becoming a potential father-to-be, I have been extremely curious about the family phenomenon, but not a friend within 240 miles has one for me to gape at.

For me, Charles is a good study for gauging the impact

of fatherhood. We have been friends ever since those knuckle-cracking days when we rowed up and down the Charles River on the Boston University crew.

After college, he kept his hair short, got a job in Detroit, and didn't languish in the sixties, as I did. At the age of twenty-three, when I couldn't even hold on to a girlfriend, Charles married an Older Woman with Two Children. Now, eight years and a daughter of their own later, their marriage is still fresh.

At dinner last night, on their annual visit east from Michigan, we told them that we are thinking about having a baby and might leave New York. Surprise! They are looking forward to the nest emptying out, to becoming a couple and moving to New York, the city of excitement. Our film, played backward.

Our romantic notions of family were matched by their romantic notions of coupledom — which they have never experienced, since all their married life they have been parents.

"For some reason, parenthood makes you respectable," said Suzanne, who had her first child when she was seventeen years old. "I've been respectable for so long I could throw up."

It was more than a bit disconcerting to hear this from my model family.

But their eagerness to be a couple, I was relieved to hear, was not rooted in dissatisfaction with Family. They just need a change. "Sara was the best thing I ever did," said Suzanne, referring to the new baby, now five. Said Charles: "Sara really completed my life."

"You have to adjust your schedule, but you don't really have to give up anything important," said Suzanne. Who then wanted to hear all about dancing at Studio 54.

Susan / Palm Beach

April 28

Now that I've admitted I want a baby, I'm curious about how other women successfully combine careers, marriage and motherhood. Today, sitting poolside at an umbrella table, I found a likely target for my questions.

"Did you work when your children were babies?" I asked the languorous magazine editor with two small children at home, a happy husband at her side and a weekend free to fly away to Palm Beach on a press junket.

"I kept my finger in the pie," she said, tapping shapely red fingernails on the tabletop. "When the kids were babies, I hired sitters and wrote free-lance articles for different magazines. I kept my name out there, didn't let the editors forget me. Then, when the kids went to school, I slid back into a good job." Her husband, a video producer, squeezed her shoulder.

Their closeness reassured me. So did her manicure. If she has time for long red fingernails, her life can't be too frantic.

Susan

May 1

At my job today, I was sitting hunched over a pile of proofs when I suddenly had a sickening vision of myself, ten years from now, still trimming articles to nestle around dogfood ads. Is this what I've worked for, these last five years in publishing? This sterile work, this editing?

Suddenly I realize I've been promoted away from the work I love doing. Whipping other people's writing into shape takes skill, but there's no fun in it for me. No fizz in the ginger ale.

How easy it would be to give up my desk with the drawers that stick. How sweet it would be to get back to writing, make more of a home for us, make a baby.

These are dangerous thoughts that won't go away.

Michael

May 2

Saw a stunning apartment today, with two fireplaces and a huge deck overlooking the harbor, the Statue of Liberty and the Manhattan skyline. From the living room we could see tugboats churning up the East River, seaplanes landing under the Brooklyn Bridge and square-masted schooners docked at the South Street Seaport Museum. *Ah!!!!* Absolutely perfect!

But not now.

We can't buy it.

Our lives are out of control, like this city we live in. We've got to wait until other people make decisions.

My job is still uncertain. Susie's job is uncertain and the baby's very uncertain. I don't know when the *New York Times* is going to put me on its full-time, full-pay staff. My anxiety about it rises daily. (I feel like a cartoon character who said, "Doing a good job here is like wetting your pants in a dark suit. It gives you a warm feeling but nobody notices.")

If the job doesn't come through, we will be reexamining basic alternatives, including whether to stay in New York or find work in a calmer, more sensual place. A major crossroad lies ahead.

Susie needs the financial freedom to quit her new editing job, which already bores her, frequently to tears. Buying an expensive apartment would foreclose her option to quit.

Plus, there is the big uncertainty about the baby. Although s/he has had an open invitation to visit for some months, there has been no response.

Already the unconceived, unborn child is causing trouble.

Susan

May 12

Weekend, beautiful weekend. Time to linger over coffee, go back to bed, make love. I told Michael that opening the door to motherhood has closed other doors. Suddenly I am not interested in scrambling for the next career milestone.

I'm tired, too, of our apartment being more of a depot than a home.

I see it among so many of our friends — he works, she works, so nobody makes the house work. Everybody orders in pizza, sends out the laundry, throws away the napkins, forgets about civilizing touches like fresh flowers and dinner parties with friends.

We've been like that forever, too, but now I find I'm repelled by a way of life that is too rushed to allow for cooking and tablecloths and wineglasses that clink.

I guess my mother's full-time homemaking — the fresh-from-the-oven cakes, the hand-braided rugs — left more of an imprint than I knew.

Michael

June 15

I think a lot about families now, but I can't sense what it will be like for us. Family tensions seem universal. My own experience dims my view. I close my eyes and look through Susie's.

Susan

June 19

I stopped in at the deli on my way home from work, and saw the owners' baby daughter. She's Chinese-American, a little Buddha with a full-moon face, crescent eyes and a fringe of glossy hair. As I moved around the store she toddled after me, crinkling my bag of potato chips with chubby fingers and then laughing at her own cleverness.

"Your daughter is beautiful," I told her mother at the checkout counter.

The mother bowed, then gave me a quizzical look. "You have one?"

"One what?" I asked.

"You have a baby?"

"No, no, I don't have a baby," I said, and then a strange thing happened. I started to cry.

I guess these months of vaguely expecting to be expecting just caught up with me. With me, and my flat, empty body that seems doomed to being forever flat and empty.

Back on the street again, I was still blinking away tears when I heard a funny sound: "Whooo, whooo, whooo." It was the little Buddha, waving at me from the doorway.

Susan

June 29
My last day at my job. Walking out of the office, I felt
feverish with excitement. Good-bye, dogfood ads. Good-
bye, desk with drawers that stick.

"You look radiant, you're absolutely beaming," my
friends kept saying. They didn't know I was dizzy with
fear.

How could I be setting myself adrift so soon?

On the other hand, now that I'm a writer again, how
could I have waited so long to make it happen?

To reassure myself that I've done the right thing, I keep
remembering — with some sadness — my last visit with
one editor. On her desk, amid the stubby pencils and
stacks of manuscripts, was a basket of golden apples,
which she offered me as a parting gift. We exchanged ad-
dresses and good wishes.

As we chatted, I saw that she took my leaving personally. "It's wonderful for you, wonderful," she repeated.
Then, wearily looking around the cramped, windowless
office, she added, "Sometimes I don't know what I'm
doing here." Her head was still down on her desk when I
tiptoed out.

Michael

June 30
Baby? Baby? Where are you?

In February, we thought that as soon as we decided to
have a baby, one would pop out. But Susie's womb is not
exactly heaving with activity.

Circumstances seem to be carrying us toward a family, though. As I hoped, Susie quit her unrewarding editing job. She's off-balance now, as a free-lance writer, but likes the freedom to write all day on the topic of her choice. If she continues to be happy working at home, perhaps she will be able to combine part-time writing with a part-time baby. That is the theory, anyway. And if she gets pregnant soon, she will have another nine months to establish her free-lance career.

Maybe that is what Baby Hinds wants, things to settle down.

Susan / Boston

July 2
My first assignment as a free-lancer, and I felt nervous as a bride. My interview subject was a Boston psychiatrist whose unorthodox technique of working with women patients is to analyze the contents of their purses. To see how he does it, I let him go to work on my bag.

First he looked at the outside of my leather shoulder bag. "It's worn. That shows you use one purse instead of several. A sign of allegiance to things," Dr. Zigelbaum said.

I smiled when he tried to lift the bag high, and groaned. "Heavy! That shows you may be in the habit of taking on too many burdens."

About my full address book, he said, "You care a lot about people." And the photos of my family's log cabin showed "a grounding in earthy things." So far, so good.

But I started to squirm when he began pawing through the bottom of the bag for loose change, a broken wristwatch, bits of paper. "You seem to have a lot of things written down here about children," he said, giving me a searching look.

With my slapdash life piled high in his lap, I sat there feeling naked. Too shy to tell him he's right, we're trying to have a baby.

Michael / East Sullivan, Maine

July 4
When I woke up, Susie was sitting on the edge of the bed looking strange. Was this the baby? Was some independent life stirring on Independence Day? Were we really going to have a baby? What would we do with a baby? Had we been too bold? Were we, in fact, crazy? But wasn't it, at the same fearful moment, absolutely joyful?

It seems appropriate that life should begin here, under the tall timbers of Maine.

Susan / East Sullivan, Maine

July 4
As soon as I sat up in bed this morning, I knew something was different. My breasts pulsated with an achy heaviness I've never felt before.

This is it. I'm sure. I'm sure.

Michael

July 28
Last week, after months of worrying about her apparent lack of fertility, Susie felt sure something was up. It was.

16

She bought an at-home pregnancy test and we stared at
it until today, Saturday, so that we could work on it
together.

After carefully mixing the potions and placing the test
tube in its mirrored holder, we sat back on the edge of the
bed, cheering each reddish-brown speck that floated down
and joined its circle of friends. A doughnut shape meant a
baby, a smudge meant nothing, according to the direc-
tions. We were supposed to wait for two hours, but
within half an hour, there was no doubt about it. We
were pregnant!

I took a couple of pictures of the historic moment, with
Susie smiling and holding the chemistry kit and acting
silly. We were punch-drunk, laughing and talking about
the staggering ramifications of that doughnut.

"We are going to have a baby!" we kept telling each
other, but the thought didn't sink in. It kept floating to
the surface, like the bubbles in our champagne.

Susie's in the bedroom now, still staring at the test tube
and writing a letter to her sister, even though she said this
morning that she wasn't going to let anyone know about
it for a while. I suppose a while is over. We are both
bursting with the thought, writing about it, talking about
it, trying to shake some sense into it. We are anything but
pros at this business. Can you imagine me a father?

Susan

July 30

Now that we're sure we're pregnant, I wonder when the
baby was conceived. My guess is about six weeks ago,
after the ballet. We went to bed and made love once,

twice. Which tumble of love, which waterfall produced our child?

Michael

July 30

It is a strange thing, saying "Susie's pregnant."

"Pregnant" sounds so medical, one of those boxy Latin words. Also a cliché for describing long pauses and fat people.

"Susie is about to bear issue" sounds too financial. "Susie is with child" is Anglo-Saxon poetry — but that's its problem. So I am stuck with "pregnant."

"Susie's pregnant!!!" I say to people I know will be enthusiastic.

"Guess what? Susie is pregnant," I say clearly, quietly and slowly to the people most likely to be shocked. Some look so confused by the statement that I feel obliged to translate the Latin: "Susie is going to have a baby." Perhaps the dazzled group had expected an "accident" report, since we had not told anyone that we were working day and night for months to have a child.

"Really?" — Brother Richard.

"Congratulations!" — Sister-in-law Pam. "I hope this takes the pressure off me. No more baby shoes from the Cat."

"When did that happen?" — Brother Peter.

"Hooray for us!" — Sister-in-law Paula.

"Marvelous! Marvelous!" — My father.

"You're not going to regret it!" — My mother, named the Cat since our childhood.

Everyone takes the news personally. Conversations ripple quickly away from our news to their plans. Women in their thirties immediately begin talking about the career versus baby problem. Men generally react with few words, but sometimes telling ones. Those who have decided against having children act a bit uncomfortable, as though my announcement reflects poorly on their decision, or makes them rethink it.

It is such a gigantic change for us, I sense new lines being drawn in relationships. Our social status is suddenly different. We have less in common with childless couples and single friends, and a new rapport with people who have children. Instantly. I feel these changes, though nothing has happened yet, no baby has been born. Younger friends ask how old I am, presumably attributing this rash act to middle age. Many men seem awed, as though I were setting off on an Arctic expedition.

Susan

August 1

Shopping this week for a place to have our baby. Yesterday I visted a hospital maternity ward. Today, the Maternity Center, an alternative place to give birth that is safer than home, warmer than a hospital.

The hospital maternity ward actually had some warm touches — flowered curtains in the birthing rooms, sleepover privileges for new dads. Somehow, though, I can't get past my feeling that hospitals are for sick people.

I think I could really enjoy going to the Maternity Center for checkups, childbirth classes, and for the birth itself. It is a pearly-white town house that was once a furniture magnate's mansion. The rooms are sunny, high-ceilinged, elegant. Not a whiff of antiseptic anywhere.

Michael loves the idea of having a midwife deliver the baby. The newspaper story he wrote on different birth methods convinced him that midwives are more generous with their time and support. I imagine that they also care a lot about nutrition and exercise, as I do. I've been holding back a little on the decision, though, because my mother had such a hard time giving birth. From everything I've read, uncomplicated births don't require a doctor. But what if there are problems?

Susan

August 2

I was working on an article at the kitchen table this morning when my thoughts flashed back to a visit with our friends in Connecticut, Bob and Beth, and their five-year-old sprite, Kyr.

"Oh, she's terrific, all right," Beth agreed, as she fried a pan of chicken for our dinner. Then she gave me a lingering look. "You know, Susie, if you're thinking about children, you really should come out here for a day. You might be surprised at how much work is involved in caring for one."

At the time it seemed like a good idea. But something about it bothered me, and bothers me still.

I don't think I want to test my mothering skills. I might find out that I'm hopelessly underqualified for the job. Or I might confirm my worst secret fear: that parenthood is a quicksand into which pleasantly familiar ways of life sink, never to be seen again

It's so much nicer to look at rosy pictures of mothers and babies by Renoir or Mary Cassatt, and tell myself I'll be perfect in the role.

Beth's offer was sound and thoughtful, and I may still take her up on it. But knowing me, I'll probably just keep postponing my date with reality.

Michael

August 2

It was an odd, odd night. David and Kathy, visitors from outer California, came over for dinner last night. As always, it was terrific seeing David, my best friend from Peace Corps days in West Africa. He and I feel like brothers — twins, really, because we have an intuitive feeling for each other.

So there I was, bursting to share pregnant news with him. But for the longest time there was no opening in the evening, dominated as it was by conversations that were essentially quakes in David and Kathy's marriage. Measuring about 1.0 on the Richter scale. Mild arguments about what type of car they would buy and who would pay for it. Their emotions, as well as their savings, were in separate accounts last night.

It was a wilting-hot night, so we had a picnic on the bed in the air-conditioned bedroom. Intimate setting, best friend, generational news and fizzled communication. This is what happens when a continent — and an unhappy marriage — get in the way of friendship.

Finally, finally, David asked if we had made any new life plans, the West Coast equivalent of how-are-you-really?

"We are going to have a baby," I said. I tried to make it a matter-of-fact statement, tuned to the key of the evening.

They both looked stunned. David said, "You're kidding, aren't you? You didn't even tell me you were trying." It was as though we were having their baby, the one they had talked so much about last year, the one they got married to have. The one they have now postponed.

It seems that having a baby hits everybody pretty hard.

Michael

August 3

A couple of years ago I did a story on the alternative ways and places for giving birth. Of the women I interviewed, the ones who had midwife-attended births were, by far, the most satisfied with their experiences. Most of them were jubilant, said that birth was unbelievably moving and beautiful. These glowing reports contrasted with the factual accounts and complaints given by women who had hospital babies. Granted, this was a tiny, totally unscientific sample of new mothers, but it convinced me that midwives have a lot to offer. After all, as one midwife said, theirs is the second-oldest profession.

But now that it is my wife who is about to have a baby, I am more anxious about this choice between midwives and doctors. On the cautious side, I want her plugged into the newest, highest-tech gadgetry, strapped down for possible emergency surgery and surrounded by a squad of internationally famous specialists. However, one statistic sticks in my mind: 95 percent of births are normal, uncomplicated deliveries, and the remaining 5 percent can usually be identified in early pregnancy. Thus, if Susie has a normal pregnancy and if backup doctors are immediately available, it would seem that a midwife-attended birth would be as safe as a delivery in a hospital.

The Maternity Center Association, which Susie and I toured this week, is a very impressive place. It has a nice garden, kitchen for cooking celebration dinner (or breakfast?), a family room with a sofa bed, a library and a very tranquil, healthy atmosphere. The medical facilities, on the garden level of the Georgian town house, are ostentatiously hospital-like — presumably to reassure couples that everything is under control despite the homey atmosphere.

The Center started this country's first school of midwifery in the thirties and opened its own Childbearing Center in 1975. It has several backup obstetricians on staff and all are affiliated with Lenox Hill Hospital, fifteen blocks away from the Center. Twice during her pregnancy, Susie will be examined by the doctors and will select one for a backup. One mother complained that the staff is overcautious and regularly drops women with complications from the program to keep its safety record unblemished. One could think of worse faults. I'm sold on the place, that's obvious.

Susan / East Sullivan, Maine

August 4

As I stepped off the plane today, a baby with chipmunk cheeks leaned from his mother's arms and smiled at me. Could he tell I'm pregnant?

Some people think that new babies have an inner radar for detecting one of their own kind in the making. I like the notion, but doubt it. I suspect that, like dogs, babies simply can sense when someone likes them.

It's such a relief to escape the concrete and swelter and return to my parents' cabin in Maine, to pine trees, loons and lake.

I waited until we drove into the private road before telling my parents about the baby. "Holy mackerel!" said my father. He twisted the steering wheel like Evel Knievel, and nearly veered into the woods. Back on the track again, he looked over at my mother, who was uncharacteristically quiet. "I'm still absorbing it," she said with an excited giggle.

Aren't we all.

Michael

August 6

Daughter or son? Both words feel unreal. But there is no doubt about my preference. I would love to have a girl, one that looks just the way Susie does in her baby pictures. A gorgeous doll with corkscrew curls, jumping out of a bushel basket to dance a ballet for her first-grade classmates.

Little girls seem so much more adorable than little boys. Perhaps I want one because I always wanted a sister, have always been crazy about women and would like to observe the species from the ground up. Father-daughter relationships also appear more harmonious than father-son relationships.

I worry a bit about this preference. What if a boy shows up?

And it seems likely that a boy will show up, since there have been no girls in my family for two generations.

Susan / East Sullivan, Maine

August 7
Morning sickness. I hurtled myself down the steps of the loft, and got violently sick in the bathroom.

"Sue? Are you all right?" Mom asked. She lingered outside the door, murmuring consolation.

Insisting that I was fine, I left the bathroom feeling stoic and womanly. But I wonder how stoic I'll be if there are lots of other seasick mornings.

Susan / East Sullivan, Maine

August 8
The baby is seven weeks old, and about the size of a strawberry. Toes and fingers are forming, chest and tummy are already there. Constellations of cells are gliding into shape in the silent space inside me.

It's hard to imagine all this magic taking place. For some reason, I keep picturing a snowstorm in my belly, a fragile white creature crystallizing in a swirl of madly multiplying cells.

The most amazing part is realizing that as I eat, sleep, work, make love, and think of many other things besides babies, the magical storm swirls on and on. It makes me feel powerful and powerless at the same time.

Michael

August 13
Alone. The quiet is soothing, meditative. Susie and the embryo are away, visiting her family in Maine and Vir-

ginia. I had dreaded the separation, but find myself enjoying it.

It gives me a chance to think of us as separate individuals, to see where I end and Susie begins. (She begins extraordinarily soon.) I have grown accustomed to thinking of us as one life, split in two for convenience and added attraction. So much have we grown together that it is shocking to be alone.

I speak to the empty room, to confirm my wholeness. I am unfamiliar with myself in this form. The apartment feels starkly empty, emptier than when Susie is absent but nearby.

Tears well up as I think about Susie, walking around, rocking our baby in her womb. I am the luckiest man alive.

Susan / Blacksburg, Virginia

August 14
While I was already on the road, I decided to visit my sister, Paula, and her husband, Dennis. I love their country life — a garden full of vegetables, a field of tasseled corn for a view.

It's fun to see Paula on her home ground, padding around on bare feet, her blond hair swinging, her eyes locking with Dennis's. Here in the mountains, she seems as rooted as the sunflowers in her garden.

I love her, enjoy her totally. I didn't even mind when she laughed at the sight of my bare bosom, now swollen to Sophia Loren size.

The baby is helping to slow me down to the southern pace. Two days ago, we started hiking to a waterfall, but I got too dizzy to climb even the gentlest slope. Then, yesterday, we spent the day at the river. It was a scene out of

Mark Twain, with barefoot boys and their dogs twirling down the rapids in big inner tubes. I was hesitant about tubing myself, until Paula, a nurse, convinced me that the baby is well insulated against bumps inside my fish tank. The rapids were no more than an easy tumble, and I loved the giddy feeling. But by the end of the day my whole body ached with exhaustion.

In fact, night and day I've been absorbing sleep like a blotter. An incredible heaviness washes over me, and there's nothing to do but give in and go under.

Michael

August 28
Now that Susie is pregnant, I am more in awe of sex than ever. Making love is recreation and (possibly) creation as well. I wouldn't want to make a baby any other way.

Welcome home, Susie.

Susan / East Sullivan, Maine

Labor Day
We got together with our summer neighbors for a lobster picnic and boat regatta. A great way to mark summer's end. My captain in the dinghy race said, "We did well, all three of us," as she gave my tummy a nod.

Naturally, Michael's dinghy finished about eight lengths ahead of the others. I love watching him at the tiller, his hair ruffled, his body relaxed and confident as he plays with the wind.

Later, at a mock awards ceremony, we were given birch-bark letters for being "Best New Parents." It's a bit

premature, but fun, anyway. I guess in other people's
eyes, we've already crossed that great divide between
Those Who Don't Have Children, and Those Who Do.

Michael

September 8
Big Daddy's birthday, number eighty-two. At the party, he
asked, "Have you considered calling the child 'Lionel'?"

Can you imagine? The poor kid's nickname would be
"Toot, Toot" or something worse. The cruel midgets
would taunt him endlessly. "It's a good English name,"
my father said, still hoping to palm off his brother's name.

We haven't found a good set of names yet. We tossed
around other possibilities from his family: Barton, Ken-
neth, Carlton Lester (that's him), Sybil, Beryl, Jessica.

Jessica, we thought, has a touch of the Bible in it and a
nice lacy texture. Jess, Jessie, Jessica: it has a varied
personality.

Being a family name, it's more ours already. Jessica
deCourcy Hinds was my father's sister's maiden name.
Maybe we'll have a girl to use it.

Boys' names are not coming. (I wonder why?) We've
looked through two books of names and none sound
right. Susie likes Christopher. It has no real impact on me.
I hope we can find a name with more energy to it.

Susan

September 10
A year ago, I wouldn't have given a second thought to
why any couple remains childless. Being childless myself,

I regarded it as a natural order of things. But today, interviewing the woman sailor Naomi James, I felt different. In between questions about rudders and races and triumphant homecomings, I found myself wondering if Naomi and her yachtsman husband, Rob, ever plan to be parents.

Their life is so full of adventure. Next summer, they will be competing separately in the Single-handed Transatlantic Race. And someday, they hope to sail around the world together — but "slowly," Naomi, who broke Sir Francis Chichester's speed record for circumnavigation, added with a smile.

I was fascinated by her hands — sturdy, square-tipped fingers that have clung to masts and raised sails in howling storms. Those hands look capable of doing anything. But would Naomi want to jiggle a baby on a slippery deck? Change diapers at sea?

In my early twenties, I used to look at friends who were already married and feel an ocean of difference between us. Now that sort of feeling is starting to come back, this time between me and women who are not mothers. By choosing to have a baby, I feel as if I've already sailed far, far away from Naomi James.

Michael

September 10

Susie and I had fun interviewing Naomi James, the gutsy woman who single-handedly sailed around the world. My story is for the Style Page; Susie's is for *McCall's*.

It would be ideal if we could always work together like this. Someday, we hope to collaborate on books and articles. But I wonder if having a Jessica or a Christopher will make this goal more difficult to reach.

29

Susan

September 11

Always one to think dynamically, Michael asked the midwife at my first checkup if I could start a weight-lifting program, with Nautilus equipment, to strengthen my muscles. Diplomatically but firmly she said no, it would be too risky to take up such a sport now.

Thank God.

I know he meant well, but sometimes Michael's image of me falls far from reality. I'm no marshmallow, but — Lord o' mercy — I'm no weightlifter, either.

Instead, the midwife suggested a pregnant women's exercise class at the YWCA. The class emphasizes good posture, toned muscles, and breathing techniques to aid relaxation.

Since our prepared-childbirth classes don't start for months, it will be my first chance to join a group of pregnant women. None of my friends are expecting, so I've had no one to share experiences with, and I'm eager for that. Getting some exercise along the way will be okay, too.

Michael

September 13

It was dreamlike, an invasion by family. They arrived with more baggage than a mule team could haul. After a fast kiss and handshake, Darcy blockaded the kitchen, closets and terrace, and Jim dashed around collecting potentially dangerous or fragile objects. Two-year-old Moira, who clearly knew the best toys were disappearing, hit the ground running. Like a puppy, she was everywhere at once. A blond blur in the room.

Our friends from Michigan had arrived. Jim, the friendliest man alive (with a face that belongs on Mount Rushmore), and Darcy, a clean-cut, no-nonsense pioneer, were the second pair of close friends to have a baby. Two Christmas Eves ago, they brought Moira, just weeks old, to Beacon Hill. Never before had a baby meant anything to me. My friends had magically produced life. Moira was the first baby I had ever held, and the first to give me a sense of that pleasurable protective feeling.

"Why don't you get one of your own?" Darcy had said, as I was baby-talking to Moira. The suggestion was over my head.

And now here they were again. I was eager to see what effect two years had had on Moira. Big effect. She is all movement, a little monkey. Constantly climbing, climbing, climbing. Tossing her tiny legs up on everything and everybody, never satisfied with reaching the goal, only interested in the process.

Conversations were punctuated with untangling Moira from the telephone cord, lifting her away from a glass table, removing ten yards of toilet paper from her fingers, and replying to her nonsense syllables.

They left this morning and the apartment seems very still. There was no question that the family looked very good, but I wondered if we could orchestrate such a wild act. And Moira had kept us from having the good talks we usually have with Jim and Darcy. Will our child also insulate us from our friends?

Michael

September 14
The *New York Times* Home Energy Issue is, at last, a dead issue. It appeared today with seven of my articles in it. Weeks of exhausting research went into them.

In the process of writing them, late at night or on a weekend, I wondered, "How will I ever be able to do this when we have a baby?" I have no concept of what changes in my career a baby will insist on making.

Susan

September 19
The midwife was right. Pregnant women's exercise class is terrific.

As we touched toes, rolled heads and rotated arms, I couldn't help staring at some of the women in advanced stages. Their lopsided bellies and drooping breasts. Funny, but on some level I still haven't accepted the fact that in a few months I'll be a lumpy potato, too.

In the locker room afterward, I enjoyed the feeling of joining an instant community of women like me. One, a doctor's wife and an enthusiastic shopper, is due the same month I am. I couldn't get too excited about the "cute" diaper pail she just bought in Bloomingdale's, but we have other things in common, including prodigious weight gains. In the first weeks she put on twelve pounds, I've gained eleven. "My doctor screamed at me," she said, her mouth trembling and her eyes registering the humiliation.

Thank God for the Maternity Center, where I have yet to hear a cross word about my weight, or anything else.

Michael

September 19
Mornings I wake up to Susie chewing oyster crackers.
They are supposed to settle her stomach, but they mostly
settle into the bed.

Susan

September 21
"I could never work at home," Fran, my friend with the
rambunctious personality, told me when she phoned today. She needs the office gossip, the pressure, the politics,
to feel really alive.

Not me. I love avoiding the subway crowds, writing on
the kitchen table, being able to make the bed or start dinner when I hit a snag in a story.

I know it sounds smug and self-congratulatory, but I
honestly feel in better company here at home with my
teakettle and baby thoughts than I ever did at the office.

Michael

September 23
Now we're past the critical third month, which means we
can breathe easier about miscarriages. I can't imagine anything bad happening, but all of this stuff is pretty unimaginable.

Susan

My free-lancing is really rolling now. Today I went up a twisty dirt road and into the woods to interview Pete Seeger in the log cabin home he built himself. A set designer couldn't improve on the way the place suits him.

He sat there looking like a Norwegian fisherman with his pale blue eyes, snowy skin and knitted stocking cap. The room was filled with wonderful handmade things. Silver tankards. Pottery mugs. Antique banjos, guitars, flutes — reminders that he is one of the great folk-musicians.

Pete's Japanese-American wife, Toshi, offered home-baked bread, Hudson Valley apples and slabs of cheese while Pete talked about the fall and rise of the Hudson River. To get people interested in cleaning up the river and caring about it again, he hit on the idea of building a beautiful wooden sloop that would sail the Hudson and prove it is still a viable waterway. "This river is your river," he sings to guests aboard the sloop, the *Clearwater*, "she'll return as much as we all give her."

I loved his rush of words about saving a river with sailboats and songs. I loved being in his cabin, warmed by the fire.

He and Toshi have been married for nearly forty years. She works alongside him on social and environmental causes, and their children's children trip in and out of the cabin. Their life seems so idyllic, yet so purposeful.

Michael

September 27

It appears that Baby Hinds will have a respectable father. Today I was put on the full-time staff of the *New York Times*.

Sixteen high-anxiety months ended with four Executive Editor handshakes. Today, I am On the Staff. Previously, it turned out, I had only been on the staff. Just think: I'll never have to write a résumé again.

I'm insufferably happy, but then how often does a person reach such a goal? One that had only recently, and tentatively, been added to the list of the conceivable.

Susan

September 28

Michael's news last night makes me so happy. For Michael, because there is no better credential in journalism. For me, because it makes my leap into the unknown — having a baby, quitting full-time work — a little less frightening.

This is the first time in my life that a man has mostly supported me, and the feeling is not entirely comfortable. I'm used to earning as much as, or more than, Michael. Now, with the free-lance checks dribbling in, and probably stopping completely for a while after the baby, I can't hope to compete. What helps me to tolerate being a "kept woman" is the thought that someday — if Michael takes a sabbatical or writes a book — our roles may be reversed.

Financial security has never been a priority for me, but now I find myself feeling more vulnerable than before.

The extra income from Michael's staff job will help us to afford a new apartment, and help support us during the months when I'll be too pregnant or too busy with the baby to write.

The news is definitely fit to print.

Michael

September 29
Sleeping with Susie is like sleeping with a bed warmer of hot coals. I hope baby likes sauna baths.

Michael

October 1
Scanning the classified advertisements for an apartment has become one of our less jolly Christmas traditions. We got into this rut by moving into New York at Christmas three years ago and finding a succession of cheap, one-year sublets. In Boston, our record was not much better. We have unpacked cardboard boxes to prove it.

Nomads no more.

This year is different. The dust is beginning to settle. My job, Susie's free-lancing and the baby. Everything is coming through. Now we need a place to put everything. We are going to find our first Home. The words "settle down" never sounded so good.

Susan

October 9

Pa-lop, pa-lop. That's what the baby's heartbeat sounds like, when the midwife holds a device called a doptone to the wall of my abdomen. First she smeared my tummy with a dollop of gel, then held the doptone, a sensor that looks something like a lady's shaver, against the place where the baby's back was resting. I could hardly believe the plucky, determined sound of the baby's small heart, pumping for all it is worth. It sounds so brave, so intent on being.

I was surprised, too, at how fast the baby's heart goes. But the midwife assured me the rate was normal as she marked a 140 on my chart, in the box for fetal heartbeat.

Besides the heartbeats, there were the sounds of the umbilical cord pulsating — whoooshing, watery sounds that made me smile. I hadn't expected a Lloyd Bridges sound track. All the underwater static made me more aware of my internal fish tank, and what a sloshy place it must be.

Now I want Michael to come with me on the next visit, so he can hear how full of life our child already is.

Michael

October 10

Life sometimes feels like an endless classified column of Help Wanteds, Apartments to Rent, Used Cars for Sale. Times when one's poverty is confronted and one's hands stink with newspaper ink. There is a certain hopelessness to it as well, knowing that the really good jobs and apartments and cars are rarely advertised. When they are, their telephone numbers are forever busy.

It is unbelievable what apartments are renting and selling for. Five hundred dollars might rent a "cozy" studio, that is, a windowless closet without closets; $75,000 buys a place that "needs decorator's eye," an allusion to walls that are caving in. Houses are impossible, starting at $250,000 for a converted stable.

We could live in the slums, and we did look there. The slums of Brooklyn are a tragedy. Row upon row of limestone and brownstone town houses. Their stained-glass windows smashed, bow fronts covered with graffiti, copper roofs torn up. Broken wine bottles on the sidewalks decomposing into sand.

We saw several nicely restored, affordable buildings there, including one Renaissance beauty for $60,000. Outside the arched front door, though, was twenty years' worth of urban reconstruction.

Once upon a time, we might have been ghetto pioneers, but this year parenthood is the only risk we can handle.

Susan

October 10
Today I interviewed Catherine Napolitane, the author of a landmark book on divorce — a subject that I find it hard to relate to these days.

I guess I've always felt pretty distant from the idea.

Whenever I've watched friends go through divorce, I've been shocked at how unglued they've become in the process. I've listened to their rambling grief and endless grievances, seen them lose their calm and gnash their teeth over broken promises and the wedding presents that got away. But even in the process of being sympathetic, I've felt detached and maybe a little superior. For me, divorce is something that other people do. And now that I'm pregnant, it seems more alien to me than ever.

I took a train to Long Island to interview Catherine, now a single parent. I had prepared my questions carefully in advance, so I wasn't at a loss about what to ask. Still, I felt as if I were talking to her from behind a smoked glass.

Catherine met me at the train, a small redhead with a sweet mouth. I liked her right away. Her husband left home ten years ago. "I remember the day he left as if it were yesterday," she said. Then buried her head in her hands as she described the painful adjustment. "I thought I was prepared for the breakup of my marriage. I'd been seeing a therapist about it. But I really didn't have any concept of what loneliness is. I was naive, a baby."

But she was also a fighter with "a terrific need to belong." She formed a support group for divorced women, called Nexus, the Latin word for "link." Soon she was laughing and crying with the others, "feeling a sisterhood."

I could share Catherine's enthusiasm for the group. My little bit of experience with the pregnant women's exercise class has taught me how vital those kinds of connections with other women can be.

What I can't do is picture myself in her shoes, slogging through the depression and the loneliness on my way to a new life without Michael. Especially now that the midwives say I'll soon begin to feel tiny twinges in my belly, "butterfly movements" that mean our baby is thriving inside. I feel so well-insulated by pregnancy, divorce seems like another planet that I don't expect to visit.

Michael

October 11
Every child I see is mine for a moment.

A Down's syndrome child, lovingly helped out of a car by his mother, makes my head spin. Identical twins, with identical cries. A girl with angel eyes — could we be so lucky?

Michael

October 19
I woke up and felt like throwing myself away. With the hangover came a flash of fear: what had I done last night? There had been a party for Suky, my late half-brother's ex-wife's younger sister and the secret flame of my fifteenth year. She's in New York, returning from Africa, on her way to Italy to rejoin her husband.

Memories slapped my face. All night long, drinking too much, fawning over Suky, ignoring Susie. Remorse, remorse.

Why? . . . I have been feeling desperate for a good time lately. . . . It was the first time in years that I had seen Suky . . .

Susie, generous to a fault, said, "You weren't yourself last night." But I know I was and I wasn't.

Susan

October 25
Some blondes are cool as vanilla sodas, but Michael's childhood sweetheart, Suky, is as hot as the African sun she just came away from.

After years of hearing about her, I finally met her last week, and took in her fascinating contradictions: the butterscotch hair and finishing-school accent along with the feisty laugh and two-fisted drinking. She's a blue-blooded peasant who kicks off stiletto heels to dance around on fidgety feet.

I like Suky — who can help it? — but I feel slightly uneasy around her. Michael seems delighted that she's left Mali, where her Italian husband does business, to come here for an extended visit.

I think I'm edgy because I wear flats instead of stiletto heels. And because our sex life will be thinning as my middle thickens.

Michael

October 25
I try to imagine our child, but can't. It worries me that I don't have any mental image of the new family, no easy pictures of me rocking cribs or diapering baby. I've got father-to-be block. It is similar to writer's block, when I can't think of a single appropriate word.

The circuits are jammed, no transmission can be made. Is it fear, that I don't want to deal with the mental images that might come? Fear that thinking about thalidomide babies, hydrocephalic babies, babies with strawberry birthmarks, would bare my inability to deal with such problems?

And yet, I don't think of Campbell Soup kids, either. Is it that I don't think I will be lucky enough to have a doll child, fear a disaster, and so freeze the whole thought pattern entirely? If so, it's effective, but not much fun.

Susan

October 26
Went to a thriving green part of the Bronx today to do a
story about a twenty-seven-year-old woman who has had
leukemia since she was sixteen. She's the subject of a new
book, which has her name for a title: *Angela Ambrosia.*

I was a little nervous about interviewing someone with
a fatal disease. *Leukemia* is an obscenity, a word I don't
use or think of often. I felt tentative about what I would
say to Angela, how I would say it. I even had the absurd
feeling that as a pregnant woman, I possibly shouldn't be
in her apartment, sitting on her chair, drinking from her
glass.

But Angela put me at ease. Small and pretty as a doll,
she doesn't look sick at all. She doesn't act sick, either.

When I first arrived, her big, black-coffee eyes fastened
on my middle, and she reached out and gave my tummy
a pat, the way an unselfconscious child might. "You're
pregnant. How many months? Atta girl, you're going to
make it!" she exclaimed, on hearing I'm about four
months along. Later, she told me she'd miscarried in the
early months. Her doctors had said it was extremely
doubtful that she could get pregnant, and that if she did,
she might not survive the pregnancy. She went ahead anyway. For her, having a child was a bid for a normal life.
She lost the bid. I sensed that it is a great sadness in her
life to have lost that chance, although she speaks of it easily, without bitterness.

When she talked about Ted, the man she married
against both their families' wishes, she was snappy and
funny. "It still surprises me to have a man in bed beside
me," she said with a laugh, looking absolutely delighted
that she'd pulled it off.

The book, by Ray Fox, tells how she spent her adolescence in the unreal world of a hospital, and how she has survived the disease, far longer than her doctors thought possible. "There are lots of stories about people with cancer, but they always die in the end," she said matter-of-factly. "My story is different. I'm going to stick around."

I hope she does. I'd like to be her friend.

Susan

October 27

Eating for two can be tricky, I found out tonight.

We'd been invited to dinner at the Castle, a fabulous home built by a movie mogul and now owned by two young stage designers. Their castle-home has yard-thick walls, tapestries, turrets, formal gardens, and fireplaces big enough to waltz in.

I wanted to dress up to the occasion, so I squeezed myself into my long wine-colored dress. It has an Empire bodice, so my new roundness just fit. Unfortunately, though, the dress couldn't hide my belly button, which sticks out like a doorbell now that it's been pushed forward by the baby. Getting dressed in front of the mirror tonight, I tried pressing the button inward, but out it popped again.

My belly turned out to be a big conversation piece. "Is it your first?" one of the women guests came over to ask, when we were having drinks in the ballroom (orange juice for me). A fresh-faced blonde, she got all dewy-eyed remembering her own children's births. "The first time is so magical, so special," she swooned.

"Yes, it is," I answered, then felt a pang of guilt because

I've been so busy giving birth to my new career, I sometimes forget about the other baby.

Later, I couldn't possibly forget. After a spicy Indian
curry dinner, the host's brother offered us a ride home. He
was a quirky driver, and soon his nervous darts across
lanes had my stomach churning. Three times I had to ask
him to pull off the New York Thruway so I could be sick
in the weeds, beside the candy wrappers, Coke cans and
ripped panty hose. Ugly. Embarrassing.

When we were finally home I took a hot shower and
now I'm tucked in bed. But I'm still feeling soiled and
wasted, like those panty hose by the side of the road.

Michael

October 30
It is in the outer reaches of Brooklyn Heights, a dozen
blocks from our dream apartment on the waterfront. It is
on the top of a brownstone, with four flights of creaky
stairs to ascend. And it is small and needs work. But we
can afford it. Our first home!

As soon as we walked in the door, out of breath, I
knew we would buy it. The cooperative apartment has
two high-ceilinged rooms, each with large windows and
unobstructed sky views. Off the living room is a tiny
kitchen with junky fixtures; off the bedroom is a tiny second bedroom, perfect for a baby.

I know we will have to replace all the windows, which
bang like bongo drums in the wind. The kitchen needs
total rehabilitation, including knocking down a wall to
open it up to the living room. The small bathroom needs
tile and mirrored walls to dazzle the boring space and ease
its telephone-booth feeling. The absurd gallery of doors in

the bigger bedroom will, somehow, have to be walled up. The horrible ceiling fixtures will have to be replaced with recessed lights and we will have to install fireplaces to give the rooms any character.

Although it is clearly a major project, I relish doing it. All our lives Susie and I have lived in other people's houses; now we can build our own. My only fear is that it will take me longer to remodel the apartment than it will take Susie to produce the baby. After all, she's had a head start.

Michael

November 6
Accompanied Susie to the Maternity Center for her checkup today. I felt a bit odd, this being only my second appearance at a gynecological examination. It's not a great spectator sport, but it made me feel more a part of the baby production.

The thrill was supposed to be hearing the baby's heart-beat, which Susie heard last month. After poking around Susie's pillowy belly, the midwife located some faraway static on her amplified stethoscope and got very excited. I pretended enthusiasm, not to let anyone down, but the static didn't make the baby seem any more real.

Susan

November 9
I've been sharing my lunch with the soaps ever since I started to free-lance, but today I got to see one up close for a story I'm writing. It was a great day to visit "The

Doctors," because they were in the middle of a tornado, and the special effects were terrific. A sound track whistled and howled. A prop man on a ladder rained rubble on the actors below. Piles of broken bricks simulated the remains of a storm-struck hospital. A makeup woman kept smearing the leading lady's face with dirt, then misting it over so she would look really weather-beaten. I sat on the sidelines, transfixed by how gracefully the actors moved around the cramped sets and adjusted to last-minute line cuts.

I was joined for a while by a bit player wearing a big pad under her clothes to make her look pregnant. In the next scene, she told me, she would give birth in what remained of the hospital, attended by the grimy leading lady. Not a surprising story line, from what I've seen of the soaps. What the heroes and heroines mostly do is make babies, or talk about making them.

I wanted to hold my ears when the scene began. Oh, the moans! The groans! Even Maggie Powers, the world's most wonderful woman doctor, was powerless to help. Remind me never to have a baby during a tornado.

"I really felt some of those pains," I told the bit player, after her big scene. "Is your part on the show going to be continued much longer?"

"Not much," she replied with an ironic smile. "You see, the show is taped out of sequence. And yesterday, I died."

Michael

November 12

Getting pregnant has really changed our relationship. That's certain. The difficult question is: how? I think, possibly, from the very first serious thought of having a baby,

there have been three of us instead of two. While it's fun
to talk about our new life and feel more deeply connected
than ever, I sometimes wonder if we aren't losing something very precious: our close marriage. More than ever
before do I realize how much of a gamble we have taken
in following our instincts.

The collaboration has made us feel very close, but at the
same time, this new life is pushing us apart as we think
and speculate endlessly about our creation, and less about
each other. The preoccupation grows with Susie's womb.
Even our friends want to know more about the baby's
progress than our own. Sometimes I miss the simpler, easier days.

But sooner or later, I bump into the idea of how exu-
berant Susie is about babies. That seems to diminish my
loss, thinking about how much pleasure I will have getting to know this new person, Mama Sue.

Susan

November 14
I met my friend Lisa for lunch in SoHo today. We went to
one of the pubs on Prince Street, lined with dark wood
and full of people who look like students, artists, writers,
dreamers. I love that sort of place.

We ordered pita sandwiches and sat there talking about
our work, sharing our news about editors who are good
to work for and magazines that are looking for writers.
Then, right in the middle of a sentence, Lisa got a funny
look on her face and changed the subject.

"Do you remember the day I called, and you told me
you were pregnant?" she asked slowly. "Well, I was pregnant then, too."

I swallowed hard, because we'd been friends a long time and this was the first time I was hearing about it. Lisa said that she'd gotten pregnant by a man she'd been seeing for more than a year. She'd had no thought of marriage or single parenthood, so had decided on an abortion.

The decision had been painful, she said, because she really did want a baby of her own someday. But the man had made things even harder by questioning his paternity and at first refusing to have anything more to do with her.

Now that the abortion was over, the man was acting closer to her than ever. "He says that he can tell me things now that he couldn't before. Isn't that strange?" Lisa asked with a wry little smile. I could see by her deadened look that their relationship would soon be over.

I felt so sad for her and the decision she'd had to make, I sat there blinking back tears. She touched my hand, as if to comfort me.

On the subway ride home, I remembered with a pang how I'd crowed out my news about being pregnant to Lisa. How it must have hurt her to be carrying a baby that she couldn't tell me about.

Michael

November 15
As I was descending into the hell we New Yorkers casually refer to as the subway, I paused on a step, inadvertently causing a thirteen-person collision. I escaped social criticism or else didn't hear it because I was chattering fiercely to myself.

What had been a comfortable life routine yesterday seemed like a monotonous rut this morning. Anxious confusion swept me away.

I retreated to the street and walked over the Brooklyn Bridge to work, and felt much better. The onset of this mood perplexes me. I have a good job and a lovely, pregnant wife. I should be an enthusiastic father-to-be, stocking up on birthday cigars. Perhaps the awesome implications of that cigar smoke are making me nervous.

Susan

November 15

"You really ought to get some maternity clothes," Angela Ambrosia has been chiding me over the phone. She said that during her one ill-fated pregnancy, she wore smocks from the very beginning, so thrilled was she to be carrying a child.

I guess I've been cautious about changing wardrobes until I was past the first few delicate months. I've also been a little slow to realize how quickly my waistline is disappearing.

Anyway, today I went to a department store and bought two pairs of denim jeans and one pair of fancy corduroys, all with expandable "kangaroo" tummies. I also bought two cotton turtleneck tops and a pumpkin-colored, tent-style dress. The dress has a tie belt to cinch it in, once I have a waist again.

When I got home I wriggled out of my tight, pinchy slacks, slid into my new clothes, and went straight to heaven. How soft and roomy they feel!

Standing in front of the mirror in my new duds, I also realized that it's fun, finally, to look the part.

Susan / Portland, Oregon

November 19
I'm so glad I came to Oregon for Greg's wedding, even if it is a bit of a splurge to fly here. Without a little ceremony, what is life? Paying bills, postponing dreams, humdrum stuff. I love ruffles and ribbons and time set apart.

Never one for splashy gestures, my sensible engineer brother wore a borrowed blue shirt, which I had ironed for him an hour before. Jan looked beautiful in an ivory lace dress that caught the candlelight.

She and Greg held hands as they repeated simple vows. Surrounded by autumn flowers, a few friends. The maid of honor forgot to hand the bride her bouquet, and so it missed the ceremony. It was a perfect wedding, anyway.

"It's wonderful you could be here," Jan said afterward, as we hugged, "but how come you're crying so much?"

"I d-don't know," I stuttered, in between sobs. "I can't seem to st-stop."

A pregnant sister's soggy prerogative.

Michael / Shamokin, Pennsylvania

November 22
Thanksgiving at Susie's grandmother's house, in the coal region of Pennsylvania. The town is a relic, a faded place over a dead mine. Mountainous slag heaps rim the rows of cramped company houses. The miners and their fami-

lies might well have abandoned the town when the coal company did.

But the people are like pine trees that grow on rocks; they are tied to this place by family connections, which dispel the gloom here. It's God's Country to Susie's German and Polish relatives, who are the kindly people Norman Rockwell painted over and over again. Plain talk and simple pleasures. Church every morning, potatoes every night and bingo on Saturdays. They are unspoiled, almost innocent, definitely charming.

Here, family bonds are steel cables. Not like in my family. I didn't know what the word *grandparent* meant until I learned it in school, and I didn't meet a cousin for twenty-three years. To me, family meant my two brothers, my mother, her current husband and my real father, who lived nearby.

Susie has enough relatives for both of us. At the table, Thanksgiving dinner is served to four generations, including eighty-eight-year-old Pop Pop and Susie's five-month-old baby in the womb. A hundred dishes, many with imported names, are aloft throughout the meal, passed around like endless communion wafers. Aunt Val, the family matriarch, offers the traditional toast to "the Absent Ones." Aunt Mim, who gets high looking at wine, offers a giddy toast to "the Future One," due late March.

Susan / Shamokin, Pennsylvania

November 23
Each time I come back to this region, where my Polish grandfather mined coal and died in a cave-in, I feel strong ties tugging at me. His wedding picture, hanging on my

grandmother's wall, shows kind eyes, prominent cheek-
bones, small features that are much like my own. When I
looked at his picture today, I was thinking that Piotr Lapinski's American dream ended almost before it began. His
baby — my father — was only three years old when Piotr
died. I love my grandfather deeply, without ever having
known him, or knowing why.

I had tea with my grandmother in her gingham kitchen,
then went next door to visit my great-aunts. I've always
been a little awed by their high-ceilinged, mysterious
house, with its black Madonnas in shimmering frames and
china closets full of brittle treasure. "Come here, my angels," said the aunt who's been ailing, opening her arms
to embrace Michael and me. She looked pale and older
than her seventy-odd years, swathed in blankets and a red
velvet turban.

Years ago, married to a much older man, she might
have borne a son, but miscarried. Now her eyes search my
body for the child I carry. I sense that my pregnancy gives
us a new connection. She wants me to be fruitful, as she
was not.

Michael

November 30

What is an egalitarian marriage? Well, no one at the Na-
tional Organization for Women's seminar on the topic
seemed to know for sure. Author Nancy Friday suggested
that it was money that pulled her equal to her husband.
For his part, William Manville said equality meant Nancy
didn't "breathe my air." A halitosic image.

Susie and I have our own air supplies and, until recently, she always made more money than I did. Not that

air or money has any special meaning for us. But I think we have an equal relationship. She does the things she likes to do, like cooking, and I do the things she doesn't like to do, like the laundry. I also prefer cooking to laundry, but defer to her superior talent. So we share the work without having to keep score.

How will a baby affect this? I've heard it said that, with the birth of a child, couples immediately revert to traditional sex roles.

Michael

December 1
Bad news and advice pour in.

"Do everything — go to movies, plays, restaurants, whatever you like to do — *now*, before your baby comes and ties you down," said a well-meaning friend and experienced parent yesterday.

"You are in for it now," said an acquaintance with older children. "Small children, small problems. Big kids, big problems," he added. A miserable person welcoming me to the ranks of misery.

Ignorance is blissful, and people don't understand that I don't want to know about the bad things that may or may not happen until I have to. Why ruin the honeymoon?

Susan

December 3
Today I came home from Christmas shopping with a fuzzy blue sweater for Paula, and wanted to see what it would

look like on me. So I pulled it over my head and then —
couldn't pull any farther.

I whirled to the mirror in a frenzy, tugging at the wool.
What was the matter with the stupid sweater, anyway? I
couldn't seem to pull it past my neck.

What I saw in the mirror made me laugh. First there
was the matter of my breasts, which have changed from
grapes to cantaloupes. Then there was my watermelon of
a belly, an even greater obstacle. Between me and this
skinny little sweater was a fruit basket I had completely
forgotten.

"You must have a great self-image," my friend Tina
said, when I told her the story. Maybe. But more likely,
it's because I've sailed through this pregnancy, still feeling
like me.

Michael

December 4

Last night we went to our first prepared-childbirth class. I
had expected the couples would be a homogenized group
of young, white, middle-class readers of *Immaculate Decep-
tion*, the antihospital book, with a few vegetarians thrown
in.

But nothing is homogenized in New York. The only
common denominator among the United Nations–type as-
semblage was their reason for choosing the Maternity
Center: all disliked hospital maternity wards, were afraid
of unnecessary medical intervention there, but were not
up to having a baby at home. Everyone hoped the Maternity Center was the best of both worlds.

It felt odd but reassuring to be a student in a classroom again. Rosemary, our teacher, is going to tell us everything we need to know about this business.

Susan

December 5
Visions of our unborn child. I mostly see a little Michael with big eyes and a booming voice, tearing at his curls as he races around the house. A miniature hurricane, full of his father's crazy energy and humor.

I think the predominance of male children in Michael's family has helped to program my thoughts, because daydreams of girls are much less frequent, much less precise.

Michael

December 6
Susie is getting big, big, big and more beautiful every day. Pregnancy is giving her face a Madonna radiance and her belly a balloon. I just talked her into putting on the skimpy yellow bikini I gave her in Paris and took her picture. What a sexy sight! She looks like a fertility goddess.

Susan

December 8
Cover to cover is how I usually read a book. But tonight I got so frustrated with a mother's torturous account of how

she finally brought a baby to term after four previous
abortions, I threw the book across the floor.

"Hooray!" Michael cheered me on. He's been watching
my mood sink as I've waded through the murky tale,
muttering all the way.

I find myself strangely vulnerable to words about motherhood now. I don't suffer the discouraging ones gladly.

Michael

December 10
The feeling of having planned a child surprises me, much
the way the feeling of getting married did five years ago.

I had thought marriage would simply be a certificate
we'd put in a drawer and forget. For me, the point of
getting married was to celebrate a beautiful relationship,
please parents, and brag to friends about our luck. So, following the nuptials, I was surprised by our increased intimacy, our new easiness together. Some unconscious
worry about our relationship must have evaporated. And
then there was the shock of respectability that this five-by-
seven-inch piece of paper gave us.

Planning a child, announcing that we are pregnant, has
given us another jolt of respectability, pride in our marriage, pride in ourselves. Damn it! We did it! We're taking
on this incredible challenge. Putting our charmed life together on the line. Catapulting ourselves into the next
stage, blindfolded. It's either guts or we're nuts.

Our parents act as though we are finally giving them
their payoff. Friends look at us with new interest, surprised at our audacity, curious about this new wrinkle.
We receive knowing looks from families on the street.

Even on subway cars, people allow a smile to crack through the anonymous, subway-riding expressions.

We really don't know where we are going, but we are enjoying the trip.

Susan

December 12

On the mats today, with eight other pregnant ladies in leotards. We wave our arms. Wag our toes. Roll our heads. Thrust out our bellies. A janitor who should be changing light bulbs stops to gape at our globular shapes.

"Your class looks so cute!" an older woman in the elevator at the Y tells me. I'm not so sure about that, but I do know that the pregnant women's exercise class makes me feel strong and good. I love pumping my lungs and working my limbs in the big, sunny gym. I love the company of the other women. We talk about cribs and diaper services and baby nurses. We comment favorably on each other's shapes and keep track of each other's due dates. Today Debra, a pretty black girl with a ponytail, couldn't keep up with the exercises, and we all wished her luck as she left, because her time is near. I'm glad mine isn't yet. I like being poised on the brink. I like being pregnant.

As I walked to the subway, a sidewalk hawker with a bunch of handbills shoved one into my rounded belly. It was from a women's health clinic, and I laughed out loud when I read the headline: ARE YOU PREGNANT? FIND OUT FOR SURE . . .

Susan

December 18
There was a lot of talk about breast-feeding at childbirth class tonight, and some of it turned me off. First there was an outmoded film, showing big-bosomed women rubbing their nipples with towels to get them in shape. Looking at these bovine women and their mechanical approach to nursing, all I could think of was cows and udders. Why couldn't we see a sweet-faced young mother, cuddling her baby in a rocking chair? I don't mind rubbing my nipples with a towel to toughen them, but I'd like to have a pretty reason in mind for doing it.

Then, our instructor mentioned something that really turned me to ice. "If your baby is blind," she said matter-of-factly, "you will still be able to nurse."

She was trying to be reassuring, I know, but the effect on me was just the opposite. I've never faced a major crisis in my life. How could I cope with a blind baby?

Michael

December 19
"What's local anesthesia?" Liz asked Rosemary, who had been describing how the vaginal opening is sometimes cut slightly to give the baby more room to exit.

"It is like the shot of novocaine your dentist gives before drilling a tooth," Rosemary answered.

Liz's face transformed into a theater mask of the Quizzical Look as she asked, "But in the other end, right?"

Everyone means business in this class. No question, no matter how ridiculous, is held back. The laughs are good-natured — we all have old wives' tale–type questions to ask. And Rosemary, sometimes straining to keep a straight face, gives thorough answers.

Liz wins the prize for uninhibitedness. To each class, she brings an ever-growing team of "support people" who will also attend her at the birth. At last count: four people asking questions and taking notes for one baby.

Susan

December 20

Dinner tonight with Suky and her husband, Fabrizio, who just blew in from Milan. Silver-haired and silver-voiced, Fabrizio met all my expectations of an Italian husband.

He arrived with bottles of wine in both hands. He kissed Michael, then me, on both cheeks. He stalked me around the kitchen like a jungle cat, pouncing on my words. His intensity made me feel womanly, and that was nice, especially now. But I doubt that I could live with the high voltage every day.

Perhaps because I'm pregnant, Fabrizio felt he needed to explain why he and Suky are childless. "Suky would have had six children by now, except for me," he announced suddenly, over coffee. Suky just smiled and stared down at the crumbs on her dessert plate.

Fabrizio plunged on, "But you see, we couldn't have children because we need to know we can leave at any time."

I nodded, thinking he meant leave Milan, leave Africa, leave all the other places they've lived during their vagabond marriage.

"No, no, he meant leave each other," Michael said later, after they'd gone and we were clearing the table.

"Are you sure, Michael?" I asked him, hardly believing that Fabrizio would declare such a thing to virtual strangers.

Michael is sure. The thought makes me shiver.

Michael

December 21
Susie waddles like a duck, but it's an endearing waddle. And it looks right. There is a natural grace associated with this incredible distortion, pregnancy.

Susan / Rosedale, Maryland

December 24
It's good to be home. As Dad drove up the hill, past the Jewish cemetery on the way to our house, I closed my eyes and saw myself, a skinny schoolgirl, struggling up the road with a bushel of books. Pausing for breath beside a tombstone. I used to know all the names on the stones, and which ones bore faded little photographs behind glass.

Nobody ever figured out why the Jewish cemetery landed in Rosedale, since few Jews lived here. With its Hebrew inscriptions and black-silk canopies, the cemetery was definitely the most exotic thing in town. Probably still is.

Rosedale has changed a lot since I was a child. The chicken farms are long gone, and a lot of pastel tract houses have replaced them. But sometimes I think the dust and the feathers have never really settled. On the road today, I saw sturdy, apple-cheeked kids who look much like the kids I went to school with. Most of them were the grandchildren of German, Irish or Polish immigrants. One of them, Matty Reckenberger, would always yank my braids from his seat behind me. I wonder what ever happened to Matty.

At our house, Mom had everything looking like a Christmas card. Ropes of red and green looped along the stairway, pine and tinsel shining from floor to ceiling. Always a cheerful house, with ruffled curtains and fresh wallpaper, it turns into Santa's cottage at Christmas.

But there's a touch of melancholy in the house, too. Greg, Paula and I all grew up to be nomads, moving often, alighting in far corners of the country. In this, we are far from typical Rosedale children. My parents' friends like to brag about their kids' settling down a few streets, or a few doors, away. My parents' connections with their far-flung children are more tenuous: phone calls after rates go down, photos from the last reunion, packages that arrive lumpy and late. I know that they are glad to have three children leading independent lives, but a little sorry that our lives have led us so far away from Rosedale.

Tonight, we all came back: Michael and I from New York, Greg and his bride from Oregon, Paula and Dennis from Virginia. Mom cried with gratitude as we all sat around a table laden with dishes and decanters of wine. I felt my own tears welling up as we broke the oplatek, a waferlike bread that Polish families share on Christmas Eve to signify family unity. First Daddy broke a piece with Mom, then he offered a piece to me, then I broke with Greg, and on and on, until we'd all traded fragments. Breaking the oplatek makes this Christmas a little like every other.

Michael

The annual Christmas swim upstream to the pool of my
conception, Beacon Hill, Boston. Everyone was home: my
mother, the Cat; my father, the Commander (long divorced from the Cat, but a regular guest); older brothers
Peter and Richard; and Richard's wife, Pretty Pam. There
was the usual mixture of hilarity, anger and madness.

All family rituals were played out. Arriving, as usual,
like a battering ram and finding our mother's house, as
usual, in disarray and the provisions wanting, Elder
Brother, as usual, put the thumbscrews on the Cat until
she, as usual, cried.

Wide-eyed foreigners tend to misinterpret this routine
greeting, and similar confrontations Peter and I have with
the Cat, as frightful offenses against Motherhood. Most
people are more accustomed to quiet emotional violence
in family affairs and they recoil at the psychodramas
played out on Chestnut Street. We tend to be *No Exit*
characters, each trying to get something that no one present can give. It's not satisfying, but it works.

Just as my brother cannot accept the long-obvious fact
that the Cat will never have a tidy home stocked like De-
Luca's Market, I, too, lose my reason in this twilight zone.
It is at once maddening and slapstick that all spoons have
''disappeared,'' or that two kitchens must be used because
certain parts of certain appliances in each are broken.

The Cat rounded up her usual suspects for the traditional Christmas Eve Open House. This year's bash, dominated by a noisy debate on the future of the Republican
party, reached the acme of inanity. Insipid as it might
sound, for me, Christmas Eve should be a time to hang

stockings, decorate the tree, listen to the *Messiah* at Trinity Church — not attend a humdrum cocktail party.

I know and I don't know why these family scenes upset me. And it's no wonder that I fear fatherhood, since, in a way, I fear my own family, at least my reactions to them. There is an overload of emotion; love and hate entangled to the point of breakdown. Susie took me to church Christmas Day to gain spiritual perspective.

The Last Supper: the Christmas turkey looked as though it had been cooked with a blowtorch. The Cat said the oven had disobediently jumped into the broil mode, all day long. The baked apples and sweet potatoes, the only dish over which she claims mastery, slipped out of her hands and splattered on the floor.

No matter; by this time we were a wasted bunch of funny bones. I served the sweet potatoes so carefully off the floor that no one's throat was cut by glass splinters. And Peter's exploratory surgery on the bird turned up some turkey meat so delicious that Richard, who had been carefully kept ignorant of the disaster, asked Pam to get the recipe. At that point, Peter displayed the bird, looking like a remnant from the ruins at Pompeii.

Throughout dinner, my father, the Commander, muttered, "Good God!" every few minutes.

Susan

January 3

A funny thing has happened on the way to having this baby. Just as the New Year got rolling, my daydreams about having a boy, a crazy little Michael, began edging away. Now, thoughts of a little girl have surfaced. If it is a girl, I hope she'll look just like Paula when she was a babe: a fresh little duckie with yellow hair.

Michael

January 4

Susie's belly looks like a sack of bricks. Gone is the perfect teardrop shape of earlier months. The fetus is a baby now, one with bony elbows and knees. (The bony genes come from Susie's side of the family.) Now and then, hard bumps ripple across her abdomen, as though the baby were trying to find a way out.

One thing is certain. It is going to take an acrobat to get out of the womb. At the last maternity class, Rosemary passed around a tiny plastic model of a female pelvis. "This is a life-size model," she said, to everyone's astonishment. My hand could hardly fit through the space between the pelvic bones. How does a baby get through? "With difficulty," Rosemary said.

Susan

January 5

I hate funerals. But today's service for a friend's mother was as beautiful as any traditional exit ceremony could be.

We sat in a spare Quaker meetinghouse that had big, curtainless windows, and bunches of wild flowers on tabletops. I'd gone there feeling a bit too vivid in my pumpkin-colored dress — the only dress I fit into now — but I soon forgot about myself in the still, peaceful room. One by one, friends and neighbors rose to recall our friend's mother: her knowing laugh and expert needlework, her love of finely wrought things, her courage in the face of cancer. Their testimony, delivered with smiles and caught voices, meant so much more than a droning sermon ever could.

Then her husband, choking back emotion, began to recall their life together. "In Cambridge we courted . . . rowing on the river. . . . I asked her father for her hand. . . . And then the children came along, and oh, the joy: David, John, Katie, Beth . . ."

I'd never really thought before about how children make a woman immortal, but I did just then, looking at her sons and daughters who sat tall and handsome on wooden benches. Their silent testimony moved me most of all.

Michael

January 8
Overwhelmed.

I go to work with scraps of paper stuffed in all my pockets. Reminders, often illegible; telephone numbers of electricians, carpenters, lumberyards, architects, masons and suppliers of an endless array of materials. Inevitably, I am missing the one scrap with the window measurements or the name of the lock I need to order.

Details seize my brain. A construction foreman sits in my head, asking questions. "Which way does the door on the new refrigerator open?" "Have you got a building permit for the fireplace?" "What did you do with the electric saw?"

Getting behind at my job, making little apparent progress with the apartment renovation. With Susie expecting a baby and me trying to show off at work, I guess buying a "handyman's special" was not such a hot idea. We should have bought something that didn't need quite so many walls and windows replaced.

In a Style Page interview yesterday, I suddenly realized the person had stopped talking. For a second, I couldn't remember who was on the telephone. Something had flashed me back to the apartment's clogged drainpipe and the incompetent plumber who charged thirty-five dollars to say he couldn't fix it. "Could you explain that again?" I asked the person on the phone. People love to explain themselves; otherwise, I'd be lost.

Susie's growing girth is a constant reminder of the approaching deadline. We can't move a baby into a construction site. I know, I grew up in one. (Actually, one after another: my mother, a portrait painter by profession and an apartment-building owner by need, has a penchant for tearing down walls and ceilings around her. When the new ceilings went up, we moved into another renovation project.)

Susan

January 10

Everything backfired today, Michael's birthday.

It started out well enough. A clear, cold day, a Mediterranean blue sky. I'd planned a party for the evening, so I had a few errands to run.

Heading for a department store downtown, I stepped off the curb to cross the street. But my foot twisted and I felt myself falling. Down down down, at first light and drifty as a feather, then plunging like a lead weight toward the pavement. A scream ripped out of the back of my throat, as I tried to break the fall with outstretched arms.

I landed on one hand and one knee. I ripped a patch out of my jeans and gashed my leg. Blood on the sidewalk, blinding white stars washing over my eyes.

The hot-dog man on the corner fished some ice out of his cart for my knee, and I leaned against him for a dizzy minute. But I felt that I had to sit down, so I kept walking toward the department store.

"I'm not feeling well," I told the security guard at the door. "Could you help me?" He looked at my middle and his eyes popped. He dashed over to the tie counter, where there were two gray-haired women clerks. I guess he figured if I was about to have a baby, he wanted some women around to help.

Quickly the women produced a folding chair and a glass of water. They made clucking noises and were very kind. I sat there until I felt better, but my eyes kept filling up. To get this far in pregnancy, and then tumble off a curb. . . . Damn my weak ankles. Damn.

When I got home I called Paula. She soothed me, reassured me that the baby is well protected. Little sister turned big sister. It worked. I promised her that I would mention it to the midwives but not worry in the meantime. I hung up feeling a lot better.

Tonight, I played guest and sat with my foot propped on a cushion while Michael served me birthday cake. It's over, and everything will be okay. But even as I write this, I find myself straining to feel the fluttery kicks, needing to convince myself that all is still well inside.

Susan

January 22
Something new to worry about. The midwives are afraid that the baby may have settled into the breech position,

which means it is coming feetfirst. Today, two of them searched my abdomen with their fingers, trying to locate the baby's head. Lying there being kneaded, I felt like a batch of bread dough.

The midwives say that around the sixth or seventh month of pregnancy, a lot of babies are breech for a time, then right themselves. But if the position holds, it could boot me out of the Maternity Center program and into the hospital. That would mean everything I desperately want to avoid: anesthesia, surgery, stitches, a long recuperation . . . ugh.

To avoid all that, the midwives sent me home clutching a piece of paper that describes a peculiar exercise for turning the baby around. A woman doctor in Bombay invented it, and the midwives say it really works. Now I've got to believe in it, too.

Twice a day I lie for ten minutes on a hard surface, with a stack of pillows under my bottom. The first time I tried it, I felt as if the entire contents of my stomach were sliding into my brain. But the next time I got smart, and did it on an empty stomach.

Lying around with my bottom in the air feels pretty silly. But if it means an uncomplicated birth, I'll lie like this forever.

Michael

January 24
I know I shouldn't have laughed — this is a serious business, having a baby aimed the wrong way — but I couldn't help it, coming home and finding my enormously pregnant wife lying on an altar of pillows.

We are both edgy, as much about the possibility of being expelled from the Maternity Center program as about the breech position itself. In a childbirth class film we saw Dr. Lamaze do a breech delivery, and it seemed very normal. In fact, it seemed like a much more dignified entrance. The baby just stepped out, one tiny foot at a time. But baby is expected to dive into the world headfirst.

In these cautious times, doctors and midwives are concerned about a slow delivery in the breech position. If the baby stepped out and his head got caught, his lungs would expand and he would try to breathe inside the birth canal. That could mean suffocation or inhaling fluid into his lungs, possibly causing pneumonia. So it is important that Susie assume absurd positions for a while longer. Turn, baby, turn.

Susan

February 4

I'm getting annoyed with Michael. "If you tear down one more wall, we're finished," I told him tonight. Not entirely in jest, either.

He just laughed and said he's nearly through. That probably means twenty more mountains of plaster and lath to sweep, bag and haul down the steps.

Three months ago, when we bought the top floor of our brownstone, we figured we'd be all done renovating by now, and ready to move in. Ha. Instead, our nest is in a scraggly state. There are huge, gaping holes in places where Michael decided to partition walls or eliminate doors. Our milk will have to cool on the fire escape, until the fridge is delivered. And the kitchen looks like the inside of a tenement — rough, ugly, with wires dangling everywhere.

I'm feeling a little rough and ugly myself. Yesterday, when I was dragging another bag of debris outside, a neighbor eyed me as if I were a character in a Hitchcock movie. "What have you got in those bags, anyway?" he demanded. I would have laughed, but it's just not that funny anymore.

Michael keeps assuring me we'll have a beautiful apartment when we're done, and that everything will be ready for the baby. I wonder. Each morning I pull on my kangaroo jeans with the elastic tummy, and go to work mixing latex paint (the kind that's safe for pregnant women), scraping moldings, filling those infernal garbage bags. But soon I collapse on the floor, panting and gasping like a whale out of water. Baby, I think you're going to get here before the paint is dry.

Michael

February 4

Few pleasures compare with digging a crowbar into a wall and pulling off a slab of plaster. It soothes the spirit, is totally engrossing. The sense of productivity is nigh incomparable, for with a few easy heaves, the whole wall falls around your feet. And then you can look through the studs at a newly created vista, in this case, of the kitchen. A few more blows with a hammer and the wall studs will be no more, liberating the formerly claustrophobic kitchen by uniting it with the living room.

Ah, yes. This urge for demolition developed in my childhood, when my mother would wake me up in the morning and ask, "Are you going to school today?"—half hoping for a negative answer, so that she would have a conspirator in her construction madness. There were always rooms to tear apart in those days. She had whole houses full of rooms, ready and waiting to be pulled apart and put back together in a Chinese puzzle of rental apartments.

Although my mother, a terrific portrait painter, never saw fit to teach her sons anything about painting, she thought it useful to indoctrinate us in the arts of house building (presumably because she believes plumbers see more success than most artists).

So we traipsed behind the motley crew of workers as they tried to cope with my mother's vague instructions. There was Hutch the magic plumber, who, if sober, could transform a tiny closet into a complete bathroom; Harry the house painter, who sang songs from *South Pacific* as he painted; and Roy the carpenter, who had too much pride in his work. Ultimately, Roy's foible caused his resignation when my mother asked him to move a wall he had already built and unbuilt four or five times. But I bet he never had another job where the boss served sherry twice daily, as my mother did.

And so here I am today, lost in a plaster-dust reverie. The dust, however, is not having the same hallucinogenic effect on Susie. So I must hurry and clear away those wall studs.

My hope is to have the major, dirty construction work finished before the baby arrives. Afterward, when things calm down, I can put in the moldings, patch up the cracks, and paint.

February 5

I started cheering today when the midwives told me the turnaround exercise worked. The baby is headfirst again. But then I had to swallow my hurrahs when they came up with a new problem.

They've decided that my belly doesn't measure up the way it should for the start of the eighth month of pregnancy. So they want me to have a sonogram, to get a definite sighting on how big the baby has grown.

They are going to bounce high-frequency sound waves off the baby, to define an outline of the baby's head and body on a video screen. It's a painless test with no known risk to the baby, since no radiation is used. One of the midwives told me that sonography was developed by the navy for locating submarines.

I'm glad that such an ingenious and safe test exists, but I still wish that this complication weren't cropping up now. I'm already feeling beleaguered about the imminent apartment move, and all the work it will mean for me. Now I have to go to the hospital to get this underwater picture of the baby, and who knows what it will show? Tonight my spirits are sagging with the rest of me.

Childbirth class didn't help. Our instructor told us that one of our pregnant classmates went to the hospital last week, because her water broke prematurely. Now she is the mother of a son. A big sigh filled the room. How lucky she is, we all agreed, to have it over with, to have a child. On the other hand, it's not reassuring to know that the first of our number had to go to the hospital instead of giving birth the way we all want to, at the Center.

After that bit of news, I began to look around ner-

vously, wondering how many more of us are destined to
have a kind of birth we'd rather avoid.

Michael

February 7
It is science fictional: a creature from outer space has invaded my wife. Textbooks say I had something to do with
creating this balloon of a belly, but that seems farfetched.

Susie's belly is so big she can no longer see her feet
without bending over. It has strange, strong effects on me.
"A person is in there," I think, but that seems ridiculous. I
look at it, touch it, talk to it, put my ear to it. "Hello in
there? Can you hear me? How is the food?" No response.

In public with Susie, I feel shy and notice some other
people do, too. Susie's hugeness is a boast about what we
do at night. Women look at the lump with great interest;
men often don't know where to look.

Susan

February 8
I can't believe it. The sonogram today showed that I'm
almost a month farther along than the midwives or I
thought. That means I'm going to have a baby in the next
three to four weeks, instead of at some pleasantly faraway
time in late March.

I guess the light period I had back in June wasn't really
a period at all. That's how I've been figuring on the
wrong due date all along. But who cares how the mix-up

happened; the fact is, I'm going to have a baby a lot sooner than I thought.

I like being pregnant. I'm not sure I'm ready for the finale. Our new home, with its black hole of a kitchen and its relentlessly grim bathroom, definitely is not.

I'd better start practicing those relaxation exercises. Only trouble is, with today's news buzzing around my brain, how can I relax?

Susan

February 10
Michael was disappointed that I didn't get a better sonographic look at the baby. It was too late in my pregnancy to see much of anything on the little TV screen hooked up to the sound-wave machine. Definitely no chance to see whether it's a girl or a boy.

I'm just as glad there was no gender tip-off. The suspense leading up to a baby's sex is surely one of life's last great mysteries.

And even without any big clues, it was exciting to try to decipher a baby in that mass of gray dots. The technician reassured me that the baby seems in good shape, moving, floating around in a normal amount of fluid, its little heart pumping. Finally, I feel I can put to rest any lingering worries about the effects of my sidewalk tumble.

Today, I'm feeling better adjusted to the change of due date. I even got some boxes packed for the move. But when I called Lisa and told her the news, she got all upset. "That means it could be any time," she fussed at me. "Do you have everything ready for the baby?"

When I laughed and confessed that I hardly have anything, she let out a shriek. Just before we got off the phone, she announced that she's coming over this weekend with a box of Pampers.

Susan

February 12

I went into moving day feeling like a blimp, big but airborne. I came out feeling deflated. Why does a move have to be so traumatic? This one was our worst ever.

First thing this morning, the moving company canceled on me, saying they didn't have enough men, and asking if I could wait until tomorrow. Rationally, I attempted to explain that I am on the brink of delivery, that Michael is off from work today for Lincoln's birthday, but won't have off tomorrow, and that I can't cope with a move alone. I was doing fine until I started to cry. "I could lose this baby," I threatened hysterically.

"Lady, lady, don't talk like that," the moving man cajoled me. He said he didn't want to upset me. But he didn't want to move me, either.

The superintendent in our building, a friendly Hispanic man with two small children, saw me crying and asked if he could help. Before I could finish sobbing out my story, he had rounded up a van and some pinch-hit movers who looked as if they had not eaten their spinach for some time.

Michael wasn't sure it was the right thing. Thirty van trips and several hundred dollars later, I'm not sure it was, either. All I know is, we and our stuff are under a new roof tonight. For that, I am tiredly and tearfully grateful.

75

Michael

February 26

Whose idea was it to buy a fourth-floor walk-up? Who was it who said it would be easy to replace the windows, install fireplaces, rewire the lights, tear down walls, put in a new kitchen? All in "a couple of months"?

I would like to wring that person's neck. Suicide is out, though. Susie would never find an undertaker willing to carry my two hundred pounds down these fifty-six steep steps, around six sharp corners. In New York, steps are feared more than venereal disease, judging by the reactions of deliverers and workmen. The two brutes who delivered the new kitchen equipment almost tore off their ears when told their company had also agreed to remove the old appliances.

I am now sitting in a warehouse where the living room is supposed to be. Thirty kitchen cabinets, stacked to the ceiling, plus mounds of wires and tools depress the spirit in any direction I look.

I've got the materials, now I need help. All my hopes rest on an Italian craftsman, appropriately named Steve Formica, who agreed to assemble the Formica kitchen within two days.

He said that last week.

Meanwhile, time is running out. The baby is due in two weeks, but there has been so much confusion about Susie's date, we are both nervous as fleas, sure the baby will pop out into the clouds of plaster dust. If you speak Italian, dear God, please ask Mr. Formica to install our Formica.

Susan

March 1

"How do you feel about having this baby?" asked Dr. Finkelman, the young pediatrician I had come to meet for the first time today.

I looked at him blankly. I had arrived at his office expecting to hear about birth weights and belly-button lotions, and here he was, talking about me.

Once I got over the shock, I began spilling out my feelings about the move, the confusion, the boxes still to be unpacked. "In our rush to get the apartment renovated, I really haven't been able to think that much about motherhood lately," I admitted. It was a relief to tell somebody that.

He sympathized. He offered me a book list. He even drove me home afterward, to spare me a walk in the icy air.

By that time, I was feeling terrific. If the baby doctor can put me ahead of everything else, so can I. Boxes be damned, I'm going to go buy some baby books, lie around like a lazy lump, and look forward to what's just ahead.

Michael

March 3

I wonder what kind of father I will be. My current preoccupation with babies has brought my own childhood to mind. I hadn't realized what a concrete slab I had laid over those early years. Now melancholy memories are flying around, undermining my confidence in being a father.

The horrible years of medieval schooling, chaotic family scenes, years of feeling second-string — all make it hard to remember that there were lots of happy times as well. I survived childhood, but it damaged me, and I wonder if I can bear to put someone else through it.

Am I going to repeat the same mistakes my parents made? Or am I going to overreact in some other way, and make new mistakes? I suddenly realize that I am not a very well-thought-out person. Only since knowing Susie have I begun to like or value myself.

I think I had better examine the mold I am planning to pour my child into — the attitudes, expectations, morality, I am about to pass along, consciously or unconsciously.

Childhood is such a fragile place. How can I make sure that my child doesn't have the same problems with self-doubt that I had?

I think I am going to have to see a therapist.

Susan

March 4

A woman in our childbirth class phoned today, and now I can't think of anything else. "Susan, I'm in labor," she said. "What does it feel like?" I asked, my heart beginning to race. She said the pains were mostly minor rumbles, and the exercises we had learned in class — variations of deep and shallow breathing — were helping.

Immediately my mind leaped to my own progress. I've been practicing the exercises, alone and with Michael. But do I really know them well enough?

As the time gets closer, I cling to the thought that if I can master those exercises, make them second nature, I can tame some of the pain and control myself during labor.

Control is the key word for me. Even though I'm as cowardly about pain as the next person, my worst fears actually center on my reaction to it. What if I start thrashing and raving and bellowing like a beast? The midwives have said all along that kicking up a fuss is fine, and I agree — for everyone else. For myself, I want a strong, serene birth. And I want only a precious few of us there to see if it turns out that way. I'd be much too self-conscious to have a gallery of family and friends on hand during delivery, as some women do. Michael and the midwives will be spectators enough.

I envy and pity my classmate who is in labor today. Envy the nearness of her baby's birth, pity her for the test that comes before. My own labor seems closer now, just knowing hers has begun.

Susan

March 10

Yesterday was so beautiful, I can't contain it, I'm bursting. Jessica deCourcy Hinds was born.

Labor was long and hard. It began when Michael and I were sitting in the neighborhood movie theater. The movie was worth watching, but my mind kept straying because I began to feel strong, pressured feelings. During pregnancy I'd often felt full as a ripe fruit, but this was new because it had a downward thrust. A new kind of gravity.

By the time we left the theater I didn't feel like waddling the six blocks home — me, the champion waddler — and I rested on each landing going up the four flights. In the bathroom, I saw it: a light pink stain, probably "show," an early sign of labor. Was I ready for what it might mean? Would I ever be?

I kept looking over at my suitcase, already packed with a robe for me, a little sacque for the baby. My mind raced through the things I still had to pack: a can of broth, tea bags, fruit, food for our celebration dinner at the Center, the camera. I wondered how I would handle the pain; if I would panic and flail and cry out.

At around 2:00 A.M., when the contractions were coming every six or seven minutes, we took a taxi to the Maternity Center, where we were ushered in with smiles. "Haven't had a birth since Tuesday," Gene said, sounding eager to get to work.

She's an older midwife I've seen many times during visits at the Center. Warm hands, soothing voice. "You want to surf over the contractions," she told me, making a rolling motion with one hand. Gliding and sliding over the pain — yes, that sounded good to me.

The contractions were still gentle waves, so Michael and I settled into the Family Room for a nap. Michael dozed but I was too excited to sleep. I kept staring at a wall hanging and feeling tight threads of pain around my hips. Icy threads, weaving tighter, tighter.

Six A.M.: The changing of the guard. Gene goes off duty, Mary, a Scottish midwife born in Edinburgh, comes on. She speaks with a lilt, rubs my feet, is endlessly kind.

Sun rolls into the Family Room, Bach organ music for a Sunday morning pours from the radio, I roll along with the pain, even though it is sharper, twistier. "I feel as if there's a serpent writhing inside me," I tell Mary. "That is very much what's happening," she tells me. "Your cervix is expanding."

I roll over on all fours, with my belly sagging toward the bed, and begin to huff and puff to get over the peaks of pain. More like cross-country skiing than surfing, now. "Is this position okay?" I ask Mary between puffs.

"Whatever you feel like doing, do," she says. "I'm convinced that women in labor know what is best to help the baby and themselves."

A bit later, I inch to the bathroom. The pains come like daggers, make me arch over the seat. I moan. From nowhere Mary appears, wraps her arms around me in a comforting hug. How wonderful to have another woman near!

By noon I'm not surfing or skiing, I'm drowning in pain. The contractions come like giant waves, filling my ears with a dull throb. I try to use the cadence to save myself. With each ring of pain, I nod my head into the pillow and try to concentrate on something else. Each time a pain comes I say a family name: Mom, Daddy, Paula, Dennis, Greg, Jan, Pop Pop, Nana . . . then on to Michael's family: Patricia, Lester, Pam, Richard, Peter, Johan, Patty, Aunt Jessie, Uncle Herbert . . . I say the litany again and again. Michael puts his hand on my back. It burns a hole there. I shove him away.

"Is she in transition?" I hear Michael ask, from a long way away.

"She's acting like she may be," Mary answers, from the end of a tunnel. Her assistant, Laura, hovers nearby with a cloth to mop my brow.

Mom, Daddy, Paula, Greg, a name for every pain. Then, a warm rush of water, a slight release. Mary and Michael are on either side, helping me to the Birthing Room. I feel like a condemned prisoner, I don't want to go. "If only I didn't feel so tired," I say over and over, my legs swaying beneath me.

Two thirty P.M.: The Birthing Room has stainless steel cabinets, a little sink, a hospital bed. Michael gets into bed with me, as we'd practiced during childbirth preparation classes. I lean comfortably with my back against his chest, my legs cradled inside his. But I can't stand the confinement of my corduroy robe, so I rip it off. Ah, better. The contractions come like volcanoes now, pitching my belly into a cone of erupting power. But how do I push? Laura holds the mirror at the end of the bed so I can see the baby coming.

Looking into the mirror helps me to focus, and I hold my breath and push with all my strength. I push so hard that I forget to breathe between pushes. "Take a breath!" Michael coaches me. I need him desperately to think for me.

The contractions come with frightening intensity. Will I split in two? Laura gives me a spoonful of honey for quick energy. *P-u-s-h*. I see something wrinkled and ancient-looking in the mirror, the top of the baby's head, all furrowed. "It looks strange. Is the baby's head okay?" I ask Mary frantically.

"Yes, yes. You're doing beautifully."

P-u-s-h. "I can't stand it, I can't stand it," I hear someone — myself? — scream.

Three forty-one P.M.: "Look, here is your baby!" Mary cries. "Reach down for your baby!" Laura says. But I can't. I only see black. I'm in another place. I don't even hear a cry.

When I come back to life, a baby is being lifted toward me. I see a fuzzy blond head round as an apple, a long ropy cord. "A boy," I say softly.

"No, no, it's a girl!" Mary, Laura and Michael all shout.

"A girl?" Somehow I've mistaken the umbilical cord for a penis. I feel as if I'm the only one who was absent at her birth. Away in another country, a dark place beneath the sea. "But she's so beautiful!" I say again and again. Michael and I kiss. Jessica's mouth moves like a little fish's at my breast. She's the color of a shrimp, her finger-nails are seed pearls, her head glistens with wet curls. My beautiful water-baby.

Later, I call my parents with the sweetest news I've ever shared: "Mom, Daddy, I had a little girl today."

Michael

March 12
I'm in a pool of sunlight, sitting in a rocking chair with a brand-new baby who smells like English soap. She is my baby. Astounding.

I had not expected anything so cataclysmic. Susie and I made love, got pregnant, and had a baby, just like ten billion other people. What is so miraculous? Jessica's tiny, perfect hand, now grasping my thumbnail, that's what.

After the movie Saturday night, I finished making our shabby, circa 1930 bathroom invisible by painting the walls, floor and ceiling black. Shortly after midnight, I laid my body down on the bed like a sack of cement and was greeting my first dream when Susie started contracting.

"Oh no, not now," I pleaded. "Let's sleep on it." But the baby wanted out and that was that.

Down to the windy empty street we went, shivering with the cold and anticipation. I was in a superconscious state, my mind absorbing every detail of the night. The nearly full moon, the calm East River, the Gothic shadow of the Brooklyn Bridge.

At the Maternity Center, I fought a hopeless battle against sleep and guiltily drifted off into a coma. Around

6:00 A.M., Susie's raspy breathing and rocking pelvis startled me awake.

It was a long, long morning, and by one o'clock that
afternoon Susie was writhing in pain. Mary and Laura en-
couraged her to cry out. That helped, as Susie — always
one to be in control — let herself fly off the handle a bit. I
sat on the bed, helpless, miserable that I couldn't relieve
her.

At this point I wondered if natural childbirth was such a
great idea.

Finally at 2:25 P.M., Susie's water broke. Looking like a
shipwreck survivor, she hobbled into the delivery room
and we settled into bed. The contractions changed. They
weren't those deep internal ones anymore; these were vis-
ible, giant cramps that wrapped around her abdomen and
squeezed the daylights out of her.

As soon as the midwife put a mirror at the foot of the
bed, we saw that the baby's wrinkled scalp was just an
inch or two inside. I couldn't contain my excitement and
babbled away about how everything was terrific. Susie
groaned.

Mary and Laura danced around the bed with mirrors,
massages, honey, water and endless encouragement. Susie, at the center of all this attention, looked positively ap-
palling. Her face was limp, sweat rained off her brow, and
her hair hung like damp straw.

"This thing has got to go," she said fiercely, ripping her
nightgown off and exposing a mountain range of flesh.
This was my modest Susie, who dims the lights before un-
dressing, tearing off her clothes like a woman possessed.

After the third massive contraction, she fell back against
my chest and said, "I'm not doing anything, it's not working, I'm too tired."

"Not doing anything?" I repeated, amazed by her ignorance of her own power. During the contractions, she pushed against my chest so hard that she knocked the wind out of me. The muscles on her legs were hard, jumping nervously like a racehorse's.

On the seventh or eighth push, the baby's head began to crown. The midwives and I cheered, urging Susie to give it all she had and praising each fraction of an inch of progress. With each contraction she pushed, and the head surged forward; each time she relaxed, the head retreated slightly.

Finally, the baby's grapefruit-sized head plowed its way into the world, and Susie's cries mingled with the baby's. I will never forget the sight of the baby's head poking out of Susie's loins. It is the kind of experience that can shake a person's agnosticism.

As Mary lifted the baby onto Susie's breast, I had another shock. It was a girl! At first, Susie thought she had given birth to a boy with a prodigious eighteen-inch penis. That was not the case, fortunately.

Yahooo! The first baby girl in generations.

Jessica, all water-wrinkled and covered with splotches of delicious-smelling cream, immediately began to nurse. She was startlingly beautiful, I thought — perhaps because the midwives had prepared us for the possibility of a blood-smeared gray baby with a cone head. Her only defect was that her ears were folded back and rather pointed, like Mr. Spock's in "Star Trek." Mary promised they would soon unfurl and unpoint.

A bit later, when the umbilical cord stopped pulsing, I snipped it with scissors. It was surprisingly tough.

That had to be the ultimate in ribbon-cutting ceremonies.

Susan

March 13

Home again, and our bed has become the Ship of State.
The three of us eat, sleep, relax, and hold court here.
Friends come and go, pots of tulips sail in the door, we
float along in our bed, admiring Jessica between us. It is
all very unreal.

You know what did seem very real? Leaving the Maternity Center. With my mother three hundred miles away,
the Center has been almost like a family, always there to
give help and advice. So when one of the midwives, who
had helped comfort Jessica during her first night in the
world, handed her over to me the next morning, I froze. I
wasn't expecting the baby's head to wobble so much. I
couldn't find the snaps on her tiny undershirt. "Couldn't
you please just come home with us?" I asked the midwife
with a weak laugh. Looking as if she'd heard it all before,
she smiled and said, "You'll do just fine."

I did feel fine on the way home, holding Jessica in the
snowy sacque I had packed for her. How flat that little
sacque looked in my suitcase — and how full of baby it is
now.

I'm glad that Michael and I have asked my family to
wait a week before visiting. My breasts, engorged with
their new milk supply, have turned to concrete, and I'm
counting on Jessica to nurse them down to a softer state.
It will be easier to adjust to breast-feeding with only Michael's eyes to see my fumbles, and easier to feel like a
family with just the three of us at home together. It means
so much to me that Michael really wants to be home, to
get a head start on knowing his new daughter.

Michael

March 13
Sunday morning we went to the Maternity Center as a couple, and Monday we left as a family. What made the difference was our lucky, seven-pound, eleven-ounce Jessica. Susie had counted Jessica's fingers and toes and seemed satisfied with the results. The doctor gave Jessica a perfect score of ten on her medical exam and wrote on the birth chart that she was a "lusty, healthy female baby." What more could anyone ask for?

We hailed a cab and headed home. "Children are beautiful, mon," said our Jamaican cabdriver, a father of three.

It was a perfect winter morning, icy-crisp and sunny. Jessica was bundled up in more garments and blankets than I could count. I kept hoping I wouldn't lose her inside the bedrolls.

As we bounced among the riverside potholes, feeling a blissful exhaustion, I looked down at Jessica's newly minted beauty and had a revelation. For the first time, I understood that boundless, consuming parental love. Jessica, it was love at first sight.

Susan

March 14
When he bounded in to give Jess her first exam the other day, Dr. Finkelman looked his unconventional self, wearing a plaid flannel shirt and lumberjack boots. He was very sensitive to us, green new parents.

"Have you given her a bath yet?" he asked Michael and me. We eyed our bobbly-headed baby skeptically.

"No-o-o," I said slowly, guilt beginning to well. "Should we?"

The very model of tact, the doctor answered, "Well, you *could*."

I really like him. Do all new mothers put incredible stock in their pediatricians? Probably. We have to, since they share the enormous responsibility for keeping our babies healthy and whole.

That responsibility has been hitting me over the head more every day. It is overwhelming, stupefying, to realize that Jessica's welfare is completely in our hands.

Michael

March 15

Jessica seems fragile as a snowflake. When I pick her up, her head falls back, as though it might fall off. Her fingers are soft as rubber bands and a portion of her unprotected scalp throbs with every heartbeat.

If I hadn't seen the doctor bouncing her around, actually dropping her on the birthing bed, I would have no idea what a resilient lump of clay she is.

Imagine the headache it must have given her, being squeezed through the birth canal. Her skull bones overlapping as she was forced out, and the top of her head looking like a topographical map of the Adirondacks. The brain is supposed to be malleable — but really!

With her brain aching, Jess arrived in this cold, dry and unfamiliar world. Her first experience was suffocation, as the air bags in her lungs weren't unpacked yet. A number of screams were needed to get them in shape.

Her hands and feet were bluish, indicating an organic aversion to our climate. And her breathing was irregular.

Raspy gasps, chokes, gags, sneezes. Expectorating mucus from the uterus. Then she wouldn't breathe at all. Then she'd overdose on air and choke.

On her third day, she got mild jaundice. Her liver was not able to balance her blood for dealing with air.

To top it off, Susie's hormones caused Jess to get her first period, one spot of blood on her diaper.

That's birth trauma.

Susan

March 15

"I wouldn't give you two cents for breast-feeding," I growled to Michael tonight.

I can hardly believe the changes in just a few days. When Jessica began to nurse soon after delivery, she was getting colostrum, a thick fluid that is present in the breasts before birth and shortly afterward, and that contains important antibodies. She'd sip the colostrum between long naps and seem totally content. I felt like a Madonna, born for the role.

Then, right on schedule, my milk came in four days after her birthday, and our nativity scene turned upside down. I barely recognize the wretched creature I see in the mirror. There are big, bruised half-moons under my eyes from nursing Jessica around the clock. There is no time to brush my hair or take a shower.

I thought breast-feeding would be sweet and easy. Gentle rhythms in the rocker. Instead, we have a nerve-wrenching encounter every two hours.

For her own mysterious reasons, Jessica likes the left side better than the right, and when I tentatively make the shift, she loses the nipple, thrashes around in my arms, sobs as if she's lost a friend. We tussle and struggle and both end up crying. Is she impatient with my awkwardness? Can she sense my paralyzing fear that she isn't getting enough milk? There seems to be a curious chemistry to this process, and so far, ours is all wrong.

First labor, then childbirth, now this toothache in my chest. It's a triple whammy. Michael watches helplessly as I lurch around in a big caftan, complaining, complaining.

Michael

March 16
I don't know where I was, not to have made arrangements to take time off from my job when the baby came. Did I think I could simply take a morning off and return to work?

Other than frantically trying to get the apartment ready for the baby's arrival, I didn't make any preparations: Susie bought the baby things, her parents are bringing the crib, and that's that. In retrospect, I see I was in a daze.

When Jess arrived, though, there was no confusion. I called a friend at work to share the good news and to ask her to pass the word that I would not be coming in for a week. It is inconceivable to work at a time like this.

Now that my week is over, I wish I had another month.

Susan

March 16
"Has she lost a lot of weight?" I asked the midwife who was examining Jessica during her first return visit to the Maternity Center.

"Yes, seven ounces is sort of a lot," she said.

The answer threw me. "What should I do?"

"Maybe nurse her more often," was the offhanded reply.

I nearly fell off the chair. Already I nurse Jessica for an hour and a half of every two. Already my breasts feel as well-trafficked as Times Square. But somehow I couldn't bring myself to say that to the midwife. So I crawled into a taxi and bawled all the way home.

Tonight, Michael had a good idea. He suggested that in the morning, when I'm more composed, I call the Center and ask some questions about nursing. He has an almost mythical belief in the midwives, when it comes to mothers and babies, and he's right. I need help.

Michael

March 17

Had to tear myself away from Jessica this morning to go back to work. But I was able to ease into the job:

Returning from lunch, I found my desk strung with streamers, pink bells, and storks flying around with babies in their mouths. Kathy and Alex wheeled over a bottle of champagne and a stack of gifts for Jess. The dresses were so small I couldn't believe anybody could fit inside. In the excitement, I got all the cards mixed up and so will never really know who gave what. Everyone in the department tried out my new name, "Dad." Much to my proud embarrassment.

Susan

March 17
Talking to Mary, the midwife who delivered Jessica,
helped a lot. From my description of the way my nipples
overflow, she said not to worry about Jess getting enough
milk. So, I'm trying not to.

I'm still pretty irritable, though. Tonight, some friends
came to see Jessica and have dinner with us. They arrived
in heavy snow, and had to stamp the ice off their boots
before entering. Inside, we provided a snug contrast, with
a fire crackling in the hearth, potatoes baking in the oven,
and Jessica tucked into her bulrush sleeping basket. Sur-
veying the scene, our friend Dick announced, "It makes
me want to find a woman and have a baby."

I was happy to see our guests once they walked in, but
I'd been in a dark mood beforehand. "They ought to be
bringing us dinner," I peevishly pointed out to Michael.
He merely shrugged and went about lighting a fire and
slipping some chops under the broiler. Always ready for
company, he never thinks of entertaining as a burden, not
even now.

I'm the holdout. Why am I feeling so pinched, so
ungenerous? Why do I suddenly feel that everyone in the
world ought to lavish food and gifts on us, and help us
with housework?

Maybe what I really want is for everyone else to ac-
knowledge the incredible change in our lives. Not just to
ogle our new daughter, but to share the strain of these
first days and nights with us.

Michael

March 18
Tonight confirmed my belief that only doctors and nurses
should have children.

Jessica was sitting in my lap taking a little water when
her throat stopped working. She sputtered. Turned hot
pink, then splotched a patriotic red, white and blue. Ambulance sirens screamed in my head as I tried to remember first aid. What do you do when a nine-day-old bug is
drowning on a gulp of water?

"Call the doctor! Call the police!" I told Susie. I
grabbed Jessica's ankles and lifted her upside down, trying
to drain the water out of her throat. Nothing came out,
nothing happened. I shook her. She looked worse.

She was not breathing and I had visions of her dying in
my arms. I dropped to the floor and began mouth-to-
mouth resuscitation. Almost immediately, she began
crying and breathing. Sixty seconds of supreme agony.
The end of the world thus temporarily averted, Susie and I
collapsed.

Susan

March 19
Suddenly the house is full. Paula and Dennis brought all
sorts of beautiful homemade gifts: a stuffed lamb for Jessie, a corduroy frontpack for me, savory soups and muffins. Mom and Daddy are here, too. They brought the crib
my great-grandfather, a wheelwright from Germany,
carved by hand. Its spokes are straight and true as Prus-
sian soldiers. Inside the crib were so many pink packages,

I had to beg off opening them all at one sitting. I'm still tired and grumpy. But everyone seems to understand.

"I'm so proud of you. You've made me a grandmother!" Mom said tonight, taking hold of both my hands. I love to watch her and Daddy holding Jessica. Their love for her is so total, so unconditional. "Look how alert she is!" Daddy says. "Obviously very intelligent," Mom agrees earnestly. Listening to the excited rise and fall of their voices, I wonder if they sounded the same way when I was born.

Sometimes, lying in bed, I feel like one of Dali's surreal clocks, melting, weeping, sagging under my own heaviness. I wonder if the purple stretch marks will go away. I wonder if I'll ever be thin and calm and rested again.

I'm looking forward to less excitement. Quiet days, when there will be only Jess and me, rocking in the rocker. I hope I'll be ready to care for her by myself, to cope with the ten thousand diapers that I'm told I'll have to change in two years. I sense that my life is turned upside down and that nothing will ever be the same again. I'm a mother.

Michael

March 19
"Satan, begone!" intoned the priest, waving a rubied cross over the sleeping babe. The exorcist, Monsignor Shaheen, chanted eerily in Aramaic, the ancient Hebrew tongue, and rubbed the sign of the cross on her forehead. Leaving behind a faint pink *T*.

The baptismal font's marble canopy was slid aside, revealing a dusty pool of sacred water. Dressed in scarlet and white medieval robes, the priest brought out an ancient leather case, with tiny drawers and bottles of rose and amber glass. With great care, he mixed oils and waters from his native Lebanon. And the Father, His Son and the Holy Ghost were again invoked, in the priest's charming accent that cracks words and stresses wrong syllables. Ever so gently, he gave Jesseeka her first shampoo.

Jerome, Eleanore, Susie and Paula wept. Technically, Dennis and I didn't. Himself moved, Monsignor Shaheen took Eleanore's Instamatic and snapped a few pictures of godparents Paula and Dennis with their goddaughter Jess. A sleeping angel, with one hand on her cheek.

For me, a pagan, it was terrific theater. There was something else, wholly unanticipated. Being there with Susie's family, crying with joy for Jessica's birth, created a sweet emotional bond, the very best of family feelings.

Susan

March 21

An important man entered our lives today. "Diapers!" said the voice over the intercom, and Hector ran up the steps.

He's a dark, wiry little man who wears a peaked cap sparkling with studs. "I love children," he told me, as he handed over eighty cloth diapers edged in green thread. "I have five daughters myself."

"So your wife uses the diaper service, too," I said.

"No, no," he answered with an apologetic smile. "I can't get her to use anything but Pampers."

Michael

March 21

Susie's father brought Jessica a birthday present: a cassette tape of Chopin, that talented Pole. "Play it often, I want her to be a classicial pianist," he said, half joking, half demanding.

He was serious, judging by his dismay at the condition of our stereo system. (It is a giant, senile contraption that refuses to play records or radio, but will do parts of a few cassettes through one speaker.)

His wanting us to tune Jessica's ear brought back some of my earlier concerns about my expectations for Jessica.

Aside from wanting her to jump around like Nadia Comaneci, learn to touch-type at the age of four, and play a harpsichord for me in the evenings, I don't know what I want. It's hopelessly confusing and neurotic, because on the one hand I fear that I have all sorts of impossible dreams for her, and on the other hand I fear that I have insufficient plans. I don't know which is worse.

Susan

March 25

The parade of tradesmen through our house never ends. On his way to work, Michael reminded me that the wall-sized mirrors were being delivered for the bathroom to-day. An event to look forward to, under ordinary circumstances. But not now, with a new baby, and my parents visiting. "I already feel like a splinter of my former self," I complained to Michael. "Couldn't we have them come another day?" But by that time the giant looking glasses were already rolling toward Brooklyn Heights.

It turned out that I was useless at the work site. With three burly men hoisting the slabs around the small bath, there was simply no room for me. I did inspect the job after they had finished, and found it dazzling. The bathroom's best feature, a whimsical Roman arch over the tub, was doubly effective, mirrored on the opposite wall, and even the ancient black and white tile caught a bit of the sparkle. I carried Jessica in to get her reaction, but her eyes fixed resolutely on the toothbrush holder instead of on our latest decorating trick.

"Looks good, doesn't it?" I prompted Michael, when he got home. He shared my enthusiasm initially, then disappeared into a corner, where I found him fingering a small, jagged edge of the mirror's black molding and frowning. "Not the best workmanship," was his grudging judgment.

My husband, the perfectionist.

Whenever I begin to feel that our home will never be finished, I try to remind myself of how far we've come. Before nursing Jessica on some of these frosty mornings, I've tapped open the damper in the bedroom fireplace, nestled some kindling in with a fat log, and lighted a fire to warm us as we rock away in the rocker. It is thrilling to realize that a few months ago, there was no fireplace there, no arching brick face, no sturdy hearth. Michael and I laid that hearth ourselves, on our hands and knees one snowy January night when I was immensely pregnant. Now, as Jessica and I enjoy the warmth, I think I see my fingerprints in the mortar between the bricks.

Susan

March 26
Just as Mom and Daddy were about to go home, my hormones began comitting hara-kiri. My whole body wept.

"She'll be okay," Mom kept saying. A veteran of the baby business, she said she felt the same way after each of us was born.

Daddy wasn't convinced. Tearful, he held my hand and kept asking if I wanted them to stay longer.

Yes. No. I couldn't decide. I loved my father for caring. I've never appreciated my mother more, now that I know firsthand what she went through to give birth to me. Stay and help me with the baby, I wanted to say. Go, so I can be alone and cry.

After their car pulled away, I held Jessica close and crawled back into bed.

Michael

March 27
Jessica must feel like a queen whose servants have quit. The past few months, when she was lying around in Susie's uterine hammock, her needs were met before they became needs. Like Queen Victoria, who could sit down anywhere, knowing that a chair was forthcoming.

Then birth, and a life of confused needs.

To need — that in itself is a new sensation for her. Hunger, thirst, wanting attention, warmth, amusement, a change of diaper or position, are all indiscriminate pains to her.

Susan

March 28
I felt I needed another mother's perspective, so I phoned a member of LaLeche League, the support group for breast-

feeding women. I wanted to talk about what's been going on with Jess.

She wants to nurse every two hours — and hangs on forever. Sometimes my breasts feel as if they're ready to fall off.

My arms are ready to fall off, too, because Jess wants to be held all the time, and cries when I put her down. So, I've forgotten what it's like to read, or think for a quiet moment. Jess has shaken me down to more basic questions: When can I get dressed? Eat lunch?

I suppose some mothers would respond by simply plunking the baby down, and letting her cry. But I can't do that. I hear Jess's cry all the time, everywhere — in running water, the whir of the refrigerator, an ambulance's siren. I can't block it out, and I really don't want to. My whole body strains to the sound, jumps to the challenge of soothing and quieting her.

The woman I spoke to was calm, sympathetic. Her baby was a constant suckler, too, and she suggested trying a pacifier to divert some of the oral energy. She did remind me, though, that Jess is doing just what she should — boosting my milk supply with her voracious nursing. The more she stimulates the nerve endings in my nipples, the more milk I'll produce.

Some of her other advice I took less to heart. She told me that she solves the aching-arm problem by using a frontpack around the house, but not merely for toting her baby around. Proudly, she described how she scrubs floors on her hands and knees with her baby strapped to her front.

It wasn't a reassuring image, somehow.

Michael

March 28

So much for our egalitarian marriage. Since Jessica's birth,
Susie has become an eighteen-hour-a-day homemaker. I
do next to nothing because there is either nothing left to
do or else I am too damn tired to care.

During the daytime, we each have our jobs and, I think,
both are similar in the toil and reward involved. At night,
though, my work ends and Susie's continues. Jessica
wants her mother all the time, allowing me to divert her
only occasionally.

The nightly routine: When I come home from work, the
house is shipshape and dinner, Jess and Susie are all
nearly cooked. Instead of accepting her fatigue, Jessica
fights it, gets overtired and cranky. Dinner is pockmarked
by screams. Jessica needs nursing, and more nursing. Susie eats with one hand.

Dinnertime used to be the best part of our day, but
now, it wouldn't be any less nerve-twisting if we dined on
the floor of the Port Authority Bus Terminal at rush
hour. We eat and drink fast to get it over with. My wine
and whiskey consumption is definitely *up*.

After dinner, I give Jess a bath and Susie twenty quiet
minutes alone. The warm bath, intended to make Jess
sleepy, has that effect only on me.

Michael fades. Susie breast-feeds. Michael passes out.
Susie breast-feeds. Michael snores. Susie breast-feeds. Michael and Jessica snore. Susie cleans up the dinner dishes.

There doesn't seem to be much help I can offer in this
baby business, but clearly, I should clean up the kitchen.
Yet at that time of night a drugged lethargy soaks my
bones. I would gladly clean the kitchen, I tell myself.
Some other time. Tomorrow. However, tomorrow the

same scene takes place. I have never felt so exhausted, so sleep-starved. I wonder where Susie gets the energy to keep her eyes open.

Susan

March 30
"I've never seen you so tired," Michael said to me last night. Just before he fell asleep.

Afterward I stayed up with Jessica in the rocker, pushing, pushing, nursing, nursing, and resenting Michael's rounded form under the bedclothes. Why can't he stay awake with me? Keep me company? "It's too much," I moaned to Jessica, who kept right on crying. I cried right along with her.

Michael's got a job to do tomorrow, I know, but so do I. My hours are much longer, and the work much more relentless.

Two of us had a baby, but only one of us is on duty at night. I don't think it's fair.

Michael

March 30
I invited brother Peter to come meet his new and only niece the other night. Other things were on his mind when he arrived. After he failed to mention the baby or approach her crib for several long minutes, I impatiently reminded him of the purpose of his visit.

"Ah, yes! Where is Jessica?" Peter said, somewhat sheepishly. By her crib, he didn't goo and gah or offer any confirmation of my belief that Jessica is the most beautiful creature on earth. At first, he seemed at a loss for a way to relate to her, then he became cerebral, discussing the life form in cool anthropological terms.

That shouldn't have surprised me. After all, my brother is a dreamer with a degree in the history of ideas, a bachelor who has never indicated the slightest interest in babies. But his offhanded reaction to our miracle did bother me. All of a sudden, I expected my brother to act like someone he isn't. Expectations defy logic.

Susan

March 31
My thoughts are becoming very surreal. After giving Jess her 2:00 A.M. feeding, and returning her to her crib last night, I suddenly started awake, and panicked. Where was she?

Not in my arms.

Not in bed.

Not — oh my God — under the bed.

Then I remembered she was in her crib. I went over, pulled the covers up around her neck, patted her bottom, and then collapsed back into my own bed.

I like to think of myself as a calm, controlled person, but I'm beginning to wonder if motherhood hasn't changed all that. Hearing Jess's cries whenever the water's running, "losing" her during the night . . . am I going bananas?

Michael

March 31

Perhaps it is well that most couples don't know what they're in for when they think of having a baby. If they did, they might pass up this agonizing pleasure of parenthood. But it is too bad that, once pregnant, couples don't learn the Facts of Life.

The Maternity Center did a great job preparing us for the problems of pregnancy and birth, but offered few hints about the far greater problems of baby — encouraging dreamers like me to think that having a baby would be like having a puppy around the house.

We've had so many unexpected miseries this first month. Maybe knowing about them beforehand wouldn't have made any difference, but it feels as if we're being mugged.

Some of the problems have a familiar ring. But the solutions? No familiar rings. Jessica cries into the night, fussing endlessly. She absorbs every calorie of our energy, leaving nothing to cushion our worries for her or our own lives. (In other words, I'm tearing my hair out.)

For the first time since I've known Susie, probably for the first time in her life, she is irritable, crabby and impatient. It shocked me at first, her borrowing these tricks from me, but I am glad she isn't bottling up all her anger. Look at us! Two wild savages with a wailing baby! This isn't what I've seen on the Ivory Snow commercials.

It all began, I suppose, when Susie's breasts, gearing up for their new task, turned to stone after the birth. Since then our lives have been stripped of sensuality, spontaneity and order. Is there any way to prepare oneself for chaos? Must we all be Adam and Eve, having the world's first baby?

Susan

April 1
April Fool's, an appropriate day for the way I've been feeling. I'm glad I talked out my resentment about being the only one caring for Jess at night. Michael says he'll try to stay up with me, while I rock Jess to sleep.

I sense, though, that he thinks of it as more of a favor than a duty. As he sees it, I'm the one with the breasts, so he's extraneous to the process. I hope I've made him realize how much he's needed now.

Michael

April 3
So many firsts this month. Her first stunning contact with sunlight. Her first brush with a breeze, from which she pulled back with a shocked, annoyed expression. Her first bath in that magical stuff, water.

First impressions on the tabula rasa.

Susan

April 4
"I'm so pleased with Jessica, I think I'd like to have three or four more children," I told Michael tonight.

Considering my mood of late, he was surprised. So was I.

Where do these crazy notions come from?

Susan

April 6
Since Jessica, my vocabulary is full of motherisms. "I just put her down," I tell a friend, to indicate that Jess is taking a nap. "I expressed some milk today," I inform Michael, using breast-feeding lingo for hand-pumping my milk into a bottle.

The new terminology actually began creeping in even before Jess was born. Once Maternity Center classes began, Michael and I were suddenly conversing about dilating cervixes, fetal heart monitors, letdown reflexes and lanugo hair. At the Center there was also a lot of talk about "nurturing" and "bonding" and "parenting," three words that still seem awkward to my ear, but that I find myself occasionally using for want of others.

It's funny to open my mouth, and hear these formerly alien words and phrases popping out. But it's a form of survival, too. When you're in a new land, it helps to know how to speak the language.

Susan

April 8
A cloud has lifted. After being inside for too long, I took Jess outdoors in the frontpack for the first time today.

Caution kept my hands cupped around her bottom every minute, for fear that a strap would give way. But how wonderful to be mobile again! What fun to look down my jacket and see a rosy-cheeked baby napping inside.

She seems to love the frontpack. I'm the one who keeps checking to make sure her leg isn't tangled or her hand caught or her nose crushed. So far, the fears are all unwarranted.

My exhilaration about rejoining the outside world must have showed, because on our way home, a policeman in a squad car slowed down to flash us a big smile.

Michael

April 9
Jessica, my April flower, smiled today. It was her very first smile, one that has been in the making for an entire month. Previously, there have been highlights of pleasure flickering across her eyes and lips, but this morning the flickers all came together for a few seconds. And a purring sound, a laugh, rolled out as she enjoyed her first moment of relaxed delight.

Who ever thought that babies had to learn to smile? Or that it takes months for them to become acquainted with their arms, legs and feet? Having a baby is an experience in human development. I guess everyone knew that but me.

Jessica is all instinct now. When she is startled by a loud noise, a shock current pops through her body and she lunges forward, with her arms, legs, fingers and toes all grabbing at the air. Trying to catch a branch, claims Dr. Moro, who first studied this activity. Some people have stars, galaxies, butterflies, named after them — Dr. Moro has an ape reflex as his memorial. Not to be outdone, Dr. Babinski discovered an ape movement in the foot: when we stroke our babinski's foot, she spreads her toes as if she's standing on a firm branch. Pressure on the foot tells her to grasp the branch, in this case my finger, with her teensy toes.

Stroke either her cheek or the palm of her hand, and another reflex action occurs. Hand goes to mouth. It's like pressing a switch. Touch Jess's cheek, zip! goes the hand. Most of the time, though, the hand first lands on her nose, eye or ear before finding the proper cavity.

When she is hungry, her mouth opens, her head automatically wags from side to side with incredible intensity, "rooting," as baby books say, for the nipple. Once, she did this while I was holding her, so I gave her my hairy nipple. She gladly sucked for a minute, then realized the fraud and wailed. She has never been back for more, even though I offered to get a haircut. If Freud had called this nipple envy, he would have been correct.

Susan

April 12
Each night I fall into bed, bone-tired. But in the morning I look at Jessica, her face shiny as a new penny, her hair fine as peach fuzz, and I get a new invigoration.

She takes so much from me that the days all dribble down into the deepest exhaustion I've ever known. But she gives so much, too.

Michael

April 12
Our house is Noah's Ark and each day the mailman delivers more species: rabbits, bears, ducks, a unicorn, a string

of elephants, giraffes, lambs, a lion, and a kangaroo with a baby roo in her pouch.

Jessica has transformed our house, filled it with odd shapes, bright colors and circus music. There is an innocence and a playfulness about it that makes me think our pre-Jessica apartment was a dull and lifeless place.

Susan

April 15
Changing Jess's diaper for the eighth time today, I suddenly felt hopeless about not writing. All those notebooks I filled with stories as a child, all the articles I've written for my jobs — writing is something I love to do and need to do.

I began to sob as I shifted cotton squares and buttered Jess's bottom with ointment. Not understanding my change of mood, Jess looked up at me and gave me a smile.

I couldn't help smiling back, and giving her tummy a resounding kiss.

Michael

April 18
No sight is more idyllic than a woman breast-feeding a baby. When the woman is Susie and the baby is Jessica, no pleasure is so pure.

Susan

April 20
The word *sleeping* doesn't half describe what Jessica does
in her crib. She presses her cheek into the mattress until
roses bloom there. Her whole head gets dewy as a rain
forest and her eyes clamp into tight half-moons. Her fists
become fierce knots and her body swims in small, determined circles.

When she wakes, her cries come immediately, as if the
effort of leaving that slow, soggy world is more than she
can bear.

That's why Michael and I don't just say, "Jessica is
sleeping." We say, "Jessica is sleepingsleepingsleeping."

Michael

April 20
The tally is in. Jessica is an Active Baby. Or so I found out
by reading T. Berry Brazelton's *Infants and Mothers*.

She is not the cliché baby who nurses and yawns back
to sleep, nor the moderate lump that makes a bit of a fuss.
Jessica is a Parris Island drill sergeant, terrorizing her
troops with incomprehensible orders, bloodcurdling cries
and an exhausting, round-the-clock schedule of
maneuvers.

I page through *Infants and Mothers*, reading how easy
life might have been if we had had "Quiet Baby Laura" or
"Average Baby Louis." Even "Active Baby Daniel" seems
a breeze in some ways — at least he sleeps four or five
hours at a stretch. The genetic lottery.

Jess has given us the six-week course in Basic Baby Training, but the end is not in sight. I look at her, marvel at how tiny she is and how long it will take for her to grow up into a reasonable human being. I pray for a sudden growth spurt.

On the positive side (never in my life have I so frequently "thought positive"), darling Jess is not colicky, nor does she have any super-strange tricks. One father told me that his infant daughter refused to sleep lying down, that she insisted on a vertical body for her slumbers. So for two months, this man, clutching his child to his chest, attempted to sleep on his feet. That story always makes me feel better about Jessica.

Susan

April 25
I shook Michael awake this morning to tell him the good news. "Michael! She slept through the night!"

For the first time in seven weeks, I've been allowed the luxury of deep dreams and unbroken rest. My clear head tells me it's true.

Michael

April 27
April is the sexiest month, if last night is any indication. The stars were in proper alignment and we made love. Brooklyn Heights moved. It was the first time in more months than I'd like to count. Good riddance to those arid months of celibacy and sublimation.

Sex is sex and much more. Is it an overstatement to say that sex is both the oil and the perfume of our relationship? Of life?

Susan

April 27
Last night Michael and I made love for the first time since Jessica. I was a little stiff and scared, wondering if I've healed enough, and if it would hurt. It didn't.

Afterward, I asked Michael if it felt the same. "Yes, wonderful," he whispered, already drugged by sleep. The wonderful part was true, but I think he lied about my feeling the same inside. I sense that what was once firm is now slack.

Another change is that sex never seemed so potent. Just look at what one night of love produced — our wonderfully, frighteningly real Jessica.

Susan

April 29
Breast pump. The words conjure up a steady stream of mother's milk. Gushes, even.

The reality is piddling. Drip drop. An hour goes by, and the three-ounce vial still isn't full.

I know I'm not Bessie the Cow, nor do I want to be. Still, I wish this business could be more rewarding. Even with the most efficient manual pump around — the Japanese-made Kaneson — I become quickly weary of the process. My nipples turn red and sore from the suction pres-

sure, and I lose patience, waiting for the dribble-drabbles
to amount to a full-size drink for Jess. Yesterday, I nearly
went mad when, after a tedious milking, I tipped the vial
over, and spilled a third of the precious drops.

Other mothers talk of freezing canisters of the stuff for
times when they leave their babies with others. I don't
think I'll ever reach their peaks of production. I'll be lucky
if I can eke out one serving a day, so Michael can bottle-
feed Jess in the evenings, when my breast supply is low.

Michael

April 30
Deciding to see a psychoanalyst was not easy.

At some barely conscious level, admitting I had lost
control of my emotions was admitting total system failure.
That I could no longer operate the equipment I had been
issued.

"Going into therapy" — a slippery, dangerous phrase.
Did I want my mind meddled with by a stranger with a
beard and a couch? What if he made a mistake or said,
"Sorry, son, you are a 1947 wreck."

Anxieties and fears are jumping up and down at the
thought of exposure. Is it better to leave them alone rather
than risk damage removing them?

The Rational Me feels it is worth the risk, that I have no
logical choice but to take it. After Susie became pregnant,
as the baby grew inside her, so did my need to figure out
my fears of fatherhood. I feel unprepared to be a father.
Now, when Jessica is at the burp stage, I feel no uncertainty, but I sense troubles ahead, when the doll becomes

a walking talker. I desperately want to avoid making mistakes, but I do not know where these damn mistakes are hatched.

I need a Wise Man to guide me through the murk. To clarify my fears and hopes for Jessica. To sort out the passions directed toward my family. To understand my lightning flashes of anger. To find out why in recent months other women have become so much more alluring to the eye.

Now that I'm committed to the idea, my head is floating like a balloon on a string. Instead of feeling pathetic, as I had anticipated, I feel tough. The biggest problem may be admitting that I have one.

Michael

May 1
My mother is a male chauvinist. Not a misogynist, but an antifeminist who doesn't think highly of her sex. Compared to men, that is.

As a portrait painter, she wants to paint only men. (To her eye, female faces lack character and women are vain beyond pleasing.) As an entrepreneur in real estate, she took in female tenants as a last resort, believing that they complained too much, used too much hot water, and paid late. As a mother, she wanted only sons, had only sons, and adored them. We reciprocated. (Until I came to my senses, I used to extract her promise to marry me.)

Our girlfriends were always suspect. The Cat liked them only after the romance ended. With her daughters-in-law, the relationships could only be called topsy-turvy.

Knowing this, will I be disappointed if she lacks enthusiasm for a granddaughter? Probably. Bracing myself for the sure letdown.

Susan / Boston

May 3

It's fun to see the grandparents' first reactions to Jessica. Today in Boston, Michael's British-born father solemnly planted a kiss on Jess's forehead. As if claiming her for his private empire.

The Cat was less formal. She googled noises of appreciation, her blueberry eyes melting all over Jess.

If she's disappointed about having a granddaughter, it doesn't show.

Susan

May 5

While in Boston yesterday, we invited some old friends, who have also had new babies since we last saw them, to a garden party.

I was startled to see how broad-faced and stocky the other two women had become. Does that mean I look the same way to them?

The babies were the stars. Ian is a little Viking, fiercely fair. Will has his mother's soft prettiness and his father's flyaway hair. I loved seeing reflections of our friends in their offspring.

In past years, we would have amused one another with news of careers and vacations. This time, we nursed and bounced our babes and said nothing about ourselves, in a garden full of cries and confusion.

Michael

May 7
Enter the responsible father. Today I signed Jessica up for United States of America Savings Bonds. Uncle Sam pays terrible interest rates, but the good thing is that the money is automatically deducted from my weekly paycheck. At the age of eighteen, she will theoretically have thirty thousand dollars, if I continue pitching pennies Sam's way.

But by then, of course, each college credit will probably cost thirty grand. Well, she can always buy a bikini with it.

I also began contributing to the *Times*'s pension plan. My retirement date is 2012, if the world lasts that long. In 2012, Jessica will be thirty-two. About half my age then, and about my age now. Unimaginable. She'll be twenty in the year 2000.

My last will and testament is also on my mind. "Everyone needs a will," I wrote in a recent consumer column for the *Times*, and added 850 more words why. But, like the cobbler whose children have no shoes, this consumer writer follows next to none of his published advice. Rather than spending the precious time and energy it takes to be a smart consumer, I take the calculated risk of being burned.

But my will story hit a chord of responsibility. We have few dollars to bequeath, but one hell of a child. Writing a will enables us to name guardians for Jessica, in the (I hope) unlikely event that she becomes an orphan. Not

*115

that there are any family demons, but it would make the transition smooth and, perhaps, easier for Jess.

In the conceivable event that we don't ever get around to making a will, with Susie's acquiescence, I hereby name Paula and Dennis Loehr, Jessica's godparents, to be the guardians of our angel. Richard deCourcy Hinds, famed Washington attorney, is hereby named guardian, and executor without bond, of Jessica's finances, and her agent for tangling with the Law. Since a will needs three witnesses in New York, let the Father, Son and Holy Ghost be my witnesses. Amen.

Another thing. I don't think we'll take any more trips in my brother Peter's French heap. Normally, it would not be alarming that his '62 Peugeot is held together with jewelry chains and shock cord. Or that its accelerator and brake pedals jam. Or that the radiator hose has a habit of spurting hot pea soup on your feet. Those things anyone can overlook. But having a child suddenly makes me more cautious, more aware of the dangers lurking in his automobile and elsewhere.

Michael

May 8
Is it that we live in the Collectible Era, or is it a universal tradition for parents-to-be and parents to save every sonogram record and umbilical cord clamp? The only baby bit my family kept was a pewtered shoe, but then my family fits no patterns.

There is something magical about first things. A tiny, tiny bonnet, a cotton bunny in a miniature apron, even a pink dress, stitched with a sappy ''Mommy loves me.''

There is also a desire to keep these artifacts for Jessica. Later on, she will be able to poke through her infancy, perhaps feel more connection with it than I do with mine.

I believe we have complete documentation on Jessica deCourcy Hinds. Photographs of the pregnancy test session. Susie's weight charts (she went from 130 to 169 pounds), *in utero* measurements of the baby and other medical trivia. If Mary the midwife had not given us the baby-blue umbilical cord clamp, we might not have considered it collectible, but now we have it along with all Jessica's birthday cards, baby gifts and foot imprints. (The foot imprints actually came in handy; we made copies and sent them out as birth announcements.)

I sense that we will be saving her first shoes, first dress, first book, first toy, first spoon, first chair, first plate, first word, first boyfriend. Until we run out of first space or first interest.

Michael

May 9
Her body is in constant motion, erratic and random. Toes wiggling, legs pumping, arms flailing.

She has no idea she could control all this activity. She just woke up and found herself in this haywire machine, jumping from one reflex action to another.

Her hand hits her face. She stares at the foreign object. Startles when the hand swipes her again, then cries. Everything happens involuntarily. Everything is rather frightening, I gather.

Her cry, though, is more her own. Once it is set off, automatically, like an alarm when anything strange hap-

pens, she knows how to increase volume and adjust the
pitch to find one that jams our circuits, making room for
her message. It works, too.

Susan

May 9
Feeling in need of a change today, so I jumped the subway with Jessica in the frontpack and headed for a mothers' meeting at the Maternity Center.

A dozen of us sat around in a semicircle, talking about
healthful baby foods, tending our children, and eating
lunches from paper sacks. One mother had fuzzy-headed
twins. Another mother's toddler sons climbed up the curtains and slid into corners. They were fun to watch, like
kittens, but I must admit it terrifies me to think of Jess
ever being that mobile.

While I nursed Jess I talked with Joan, a new mother
sitting near me. Her cornflower-blue eyes are deeply shad-
owed — no sleeping through the night for her. She's a
former book editor and Andrew, her first child, is around
Jess's age, so we have lots in common.

I've been eager to meet another mother to share time
with, and it turns out Joan lives nearby. Already we've
talked about taking the babes for walks in the park. I'm
hoping we can also swap baby-sitting stints, to give each
other a little time off. Maybe I'll be less lonely, now that I
know Joan.

Michael

May 10
When Jessica wakes from sleep she always cries. Even before her eyes open and before she knows her mother is missing. Perhaps hunger has interrupted her dream, perhaps she senses sleep and dream ebbing.

I feel the same way many mornings, but don't know enough to cry. I wonder when and why this useful trait was lost. It seems so cathartic.

Susan

May 10
"Is that a baby you've got in there?" Tom, our neighborhood vagrant, asked me today.

I stepped closer to his whiskers and tatters, and opened the frontpack so he could see Jessica's face.

Tom leaned against his shopping cart full of possessions, stared at Jess for a long moment, and said, "You're lucky."

Susan

May 15
The first-floor tenant forgot her key and came in the late afternoon to make a phone call. I was still wandering around with uncombed hair, my blouse unbuttoned so that Jess could have instant access to her milk supply.

In her eyes I saw amusement, and some disbelief. She may have been comparing me to my old self, when I toted a fancy briefcase, and breezed off to press conferences.

No matter. I was dying to talk to someone, so I pressed a glass of juice into her hand and tied her up in conversation for as long as I possibly could.

I doubt she understood my need to talk, or the reasons why my life is so chaotic now. Why should she? She's not a new mother.

Susan / *Shamokin, Pennsylvania*

May 17
I thought bringing Jessica back to the coal country would be fun for all of us. My relatives' enthusiasm for her was enjoyable, all right, but the trip has been too much like work.

Jess was passed from hand to hand by grandparents and great-aunts, and photographed each time, like a trophy fish. Her eyes popped whenever the camera flashed, and her fussiness increased as the photo sessions wore on.

By the end of the day she was inconsolable, and I was a wreck. I mumbled something incoherent to the family as I carried a dinner tray up to the bedroom, where Jess and I passed out over our respective meals.

Sharing a baby with extended family is a nice idea, but the reality is something else. Maybe I'm just not ready for the combined rigors of travel and motherhood.

Michael

May 19
For the first couple of months, Susie never nursed Jessica in public. It was still an experimental procedure. Modest

Susie, who wears slips under the most opaque dresses, still felt more woman than mother.

She is all mother now, as a result of Jessica's almost constant thirst. Jessica is a permanent appendage at her breast. The in-between-feeding times are so short that Susie sometimes walks around the house bare-chested, too tired to put herself back together again.

A side effect of motherhood is that Susie is in closer touch with her body. I like her new naturalness. By the time Jessica has quenched her thirst, I may be able to throw out those slips.

Susan

May 19
What do you do with a baby?

I know about nursing and rocking and diapering and bathing and tickling. But, what else?

Jessica is too little for ring-around-a-rosy or Simon Says. She's not much interested in books, although I've tried showing her simple pictures of smiling faces and bright-colored animals. Music gets no special reaction from her, either, even when it's accompanied by a quintet of toy giraffes, dangling from the musical mobile over her crib.

I guess I'm too impatient. I want to read to her, sing with her, paint splashy watercolor pictures side by side. In the meantime, I wake up each morning asking myself the same question: What do you do with a baby?

Michael

May 20

I am committed to the idea of starting therapy, but I
haven't decided how to feel about it. Is it something I
shall tell my friends? I try it out on Georgia, my best
friend at work.

"I think that's terrific!" she said. "Hey, Nadine!" she
called across the office corridor. "Michael's going into
therapy to work out his feelings about being a father."
Thus eliminating the possibility that this would be our little secret. Also making me feel that it was not something
to whisper about or be ashamed of.

"You're going into therapy just for that? I've never
heard of such a thing," Nadine said.

Susan

May 20

It's a boost to the ego, being a "model couple." At the
midwives' invitation, we went back to the Maternity Center to tell a group of expectant couples about our first two
months with Jessica.

As we carried Jess into the room, I could feel the couples straining forward to see her. They couldn't tear their
eyes away from her fluff of apricot hair, her tiny form
inside terry-cloth sleepers. One shameless mother-to-be
kept waving and winking at her. A prospective father
laughed and laughed when Jess let out a tiny sneeze. In
their enraptured faces, I could see their expectations of
their own babies.

Before long, Jess began to cry, and I slipped open my
dress top and let her nurse. "You look so comfortable

doing that!'' one woman complimented me. I tried to describe the learning process that had led to our good nursing relationship now.

But what the couples mostly wanted to hear about was the birth itself. And why not? That was all I could think of, when I was expecting. Mentally, it seems difficult, if not impossible, for parents-to-be to jump ahead to breast-feeding and child care and other realities that lie just beyond the big hurdle of giving birth.

Without much urging, Michael and I launched into the saga of March 9. The Bach organ music, the big, bad pushing stage, the cord-cutting ceremony. Our voices kept wavering with emotion as we took turns telling different slices of the story.

When we got home, we were still riding an emotional high. "I think it was good for us to do that," I told Michael. He agreed that with all the work a baby brings, it is too easy to lose the wonder that we relived tonight.

Michael / Chicago

May 23

In town to do a story about the first solar home built in America, and, as a dividend, to see two friends.

Sam and Michael, my hosts and former colleagues at a New Jersey newspaper, started me off with beers in a bar owned and operated by bona fide midgets, then lava-hot seafood in a Spanish restaurant decorated with pink plastic fishnets. Afterward, a tour of rock and jazz clubs filled with singles and pickup hustle.

Thrown back to this world, it was easy to forget about Jessica. But once she was remembered, there was no stopping the memories. At Michael's, we talked long into the night. "I can't believe you've got a daughter," both friends kept saying. I can barely believe it myself.

Susan

May 27

Michael forgot my birthday today. I really felt I needed a ribboned package, a little ceremony. But nothing happened.

I feel numb about it. I keep thinking of my mother. I remember her telling me that when she was doing two jobs one difficult year, teaching school by day and caring for my brother and me at night, my father forgot her birthday. How crushed she was, how unappreciated she felt.

I wonder why my father forgot my mother's birthday. I wonder why Michael forgot mine.

Michael

May 27

How could I have forgotten Susie's birthday? For months I've kept an eye on store windows and advertisements, looking for the perfect gift. I made tentative plans to dine out, go to the ballet. Then in the last couple of weeks, the birthday slipped out of mind. Until the Happy Birthday calls started ringing in tonight.

I don't know what's happening. I must be losing my mind, is all I can think. My energy level is not measurable. My brain is hardly making waves.

If I go to work with less than eight perfect hours of sleep, I am useless there, too. I look at the lists of people I

need to interview for a story and call home instead. Trying
to get an injection of enthusiasm from Susie.

Keeping up with baby takes a lot of energy. I wish I
could hang a solar panel on my back and a windmill on
my cap.

Susan

May 29

In a flood of embarrassment, Michael remembered my
birthday — and bought out Bloomingdale's. There's a
raspberry bathing suit, a pink bath coat, a white lace evening dress.

The gifts don't make up for Michael's forgetfulness. I
still feel numb about that. But for his sake I've been pretending that all is well again. To show my enthusiasm, I
even wore the evening dress to some friends' house, when
they asked us over for coffee.

Sitting in their kitchen in faded jeans, our friends
seemed stunned to see me in lace. But unlike my former
self, I didn't feel at all self-conscious. I guess having a
baby has loosened me up in more ways than one.

Michael

May 30

Consciousness has dawned in Jessica's right hand. From
her first breath, it seems, she clenched and unclenched
that right hand. Then, a few days ago, she noticed its
movement and became enthralled with it. Some innate
desire to master this trick sent off tracers through her bil-

lion brain cells, looking for the particular switch that controls this movement.

Today, she found the switch and began operating it with abandon. Her control is minimal; any distraction short-circuits it.

But her body is a self-instructing organism, involuntarily clenching and unclenching the hand, telling Jessica: "Find me and turn me off." So, again, the tracer goes out, scanning the circuits, finding the right-hand switch deep in her cerebellum. Each search is quicker than the previous one; sooner or later, she won't have to look.

The first synapse is mastered. Only about a million more remain to be pioneered.

Susan

May 30

A former neighbor who is a bachelor came by today with a tulip-trimmed sunsuit for Jessica, and stayed for tea.

"Did you plan on this? Were you ready to have a baby?" he asked nonchalantly.

I looked up from the sunsuit, which I had been admiring, and didn't know how to answer him.

"Don't we look ready?" I dodged the question, waving my arm vaguely at Jessica's sleeping basket, stuffed animals, stack of diapers. Our friend laughed, his interrogation derailed.

A more truthful answer would have been: We thought we were ready. We thought we knew what ready was. But that burst of baby named Jessica hit our lives like TNT, and ever since we've been in a daze. With ears ringing and eyes searching for reinforcements.

Michael

May 31
Psychiatrist? Behaviorist? Primal Screamer? Picking the right flavor of therapy is perplexing.

A friend at the *Times* recommended Howard Kogan. "He is a friendly bear of a guy, like Judd Hirsch in *Ordinary People*. He talks, too."

I certainly want one that talks, and one that talks well. I called Howard up, trying to sound casual but feeling as if I were making an appointment for a sex-change operation. His response strengthened the feeling.

"Come to the eleventh floor of the Kidney Center Building," he said softly. "Have a seat in the waiting room until I come get you."

Okay . . .

On the eleventh floor, thinking about my kidneys. The waiting room is designed to turn the eyes inward: the major decorative elements are a phosphorescent astrology poster, a mangy plastic plant and a profusion of blackened aluminum ashtrays. NO SMOKING! says a sign in the adjacent office. Mixed signals everywhere, even in the Kidney Center building for shrinks. The secretaries, protected behind glass windows, look up at me, show no expression, look away. The New York City Survival Look.

At the appointed hour, Howard approaches, rescues me from the ashtrays and secretaries. He speed-reads my letter, in which I summarized my chaotic childhood, self-doubts, volcanic anger, inappropriately directed attentions to women friends like Suky, and concern about being a father. A little tune-up, please, I ask.

These are not simple issues, Howard says gently. It will take a lot of time, a lot of talking. Months, a year, maybe two. In shock, I hear him say that my fears about ruining Jessica's life seem to be mirror images of my own unhealed childhood wounds. He says that the child in me is identifying with Jessica, anticipating for her the pains I felt, the rage against my family, the unhappiness with myself.

That a sudden, highly inconvenient attraction for other women shows anger against Susie, my mother and myself. That my sudden bursts of anger and lingering self-doubts may also be related to unreconciled feelings about my mother. My mother was really getting it on the jaw.

To gain confidence in my relationship with Jessica, and to figure out what my expectations for her are, means understanding myself, Howard says. To do that we will track every problem back to its childhood origins, he adds.

Aye yi yi, I say. But secretly, I am relieved.

Howard seems positively eager to get to work on the puzzle, and as I leave the Kidney Center, my organs feel infinitely better. He understood my problems, was sharing the burden. And they are resolvable problems. I feel great changes coming.

Susan

May 31

I'm a little squeamish about being dissected by Michael and Howard, his new therapist. "Did you talk about me at all?" I dared to ask Michael, after he came back from his first session.

Michael laughed and said he told Howard only good things about me. Then he said that since Howard has agreed to let him tape the sessions on his pocket-size recorder from now on, I can listen to any that I choose.

I doubt that I would make the same offer, if I were the one in therapy. I love Michael for being so open. Maybe we'll both learn from this experience.

Susan

June 3

I'm finding that outsiders have the wrong idea about my situation.

"You must be getting a lot of writing done," said a childless friend who works in publishing. "Little babies sleep a lot, don't they?"

Yes, sure, I told her. Some babies do. But not mine.

Except for this diary, which I scribble in while Jess is nursing or snuggling in the crook of my left arm, I haven't written a word since she was born.

Michael

June 5

Assigned a "funny" story on a three-hour adult-education course on how to pick up women. It turned out to be an extremely depressing assignment. Poor guys taking the course were hypertimid, introverted, emotionally or physically warped. The only "funny" thing that happened was that one of the students tried to pick me up, using one of the hot first lines ("Don't I know you from somewhere?") he had just learned.

It was the kind of night, akin to visiting the emergency ward in a children's hospital, that puts all of one's problems into perspective.

Michael

June 6
"What do you want to give Jessica?" asked Howard.

"A chance to be fully aware of all the options and know that she can handle any of them," I answered. I want her to be dauntless. Not hang on other people's view of herself. Strike out on her own for whatever she wants. And definitely, not drag a sea anchor of self-doubts behind her. In other words, not follow in her father's footsteps.

"How are you going to give that to her?" Howard asked.

"I'm not sure. I am afraid I might not be able to, because I have no idea how I got so hung up," I said.

The archaeological process has begun. Finding the answers for Jessica means finding out about myself.

Each fragment of my life is exhumed, examined, marked and shelved. Hopefully, when all the pieces are assembled, a whole person will be recovered. Never did I think going to see a therapist for Jessica's sake would pay such big dividends for me.

Susan

June 6
It was a rosy evening, so Michael, Jess and I walked along the Promenade to enjoy the sunset and the breezes off the river. We stopped to watch a fashion photo session that was under way along our path.

The female model, a dazzling creature done up in silk, pointed to Jessica in her sailor hat and said, "She's the one who ought to be photographed."

Michael

June 7

It is lucky that Jessica is so damn beautiful. Otherwise, I might have abandoned her at the foot of the Statue of Liberty by now.

It is morning. Sleep has dried last night's tears and reset the pendulum of her mood. Daily, the pendulum swings from exhilaration to "ego disintegration," the words Anna Freud used to describe the baby's end-of-day crises, which we know so well. Unfortunately, the baby's ego is not the only one that disintegrates — all nearby egos melt down.

But now, for a priceless moment, Jessica sits calmly in my lap, still dazed by sleep. She holds a hand up in the air, making a flowery gesture that Renaissance artists used to portray the Christ-child offering a blessing. Jessica has a repertoire of these arrested motions, each a pose, each a flash photograph.

Except for a freckle that recently appeared on her left ankle, she is flawless. Cobalt blue eyes, parchment skin dabbed with rouge, a bald top with apricot curls in a Benjamin Franklin do.

Pride. I never knew it could be such a hot, purifying feeling. A look at Jessica is all it takes.

Susan

June 9

Not earning my own money bothers me. After all these years of bringing home a paycheck, I'm finding it disorienting to draw from the till and put nothing back. I try not to look into shop windows for fear of seeing something enticing. I wince as each family birthday looms, knowing that Michael will be footing the bill for the gifts.

Always generous, he seemed genuinely surprised when I mentioned my feelings. "What difference does it make whose money it is?" is his attitude.

I'd like to feel the same way. It's disconcerting to realize that I'm so much a product of the rat race, I've swallowed its values whole.

Susan

June 10

Joan and I began swap baby-sitting today, when I took Andrew for the morning, and what an experience! How do other mothers ever get brave enough to have two?

It sounds sexist, but Andrew is so much more taut and muscular than Jess, who's a pillow by comparison. Andrew is also more athletic, already able to roll himself off a couch, or tilt suddenly toward the floor. With two babies to watch I had my hands full, literally.

Before Joan left, we discussed breast-feeding each other's babies, and we agreed to do it if the need arose. In Andrew's case the need arose almost immediately. He began to howl, and wouldn't be appeased by a bottle. A bit timidly I offered my breast. He suckled and pumped much more aggressively than Jess ever does, pushing back and forth with his hands to increase his pumping power. Another sex difference that seems too pat to be true.

After shifting two babies off the sofa, into my arms and onto the breast in dizzy succession, I began to wonder how well baby-swapping is going to work out. I'll need all day tomorrow to recover.

Michael

June 13
At Howard's, I discovered one reason why I feel so at sea with this business of fatherhood: I have no strong role model, no good reference point in my own life.

I sense I'm molding Jessica's personality in subtle ways, but don't know what the mold looks like myself, I told Howard. Certainly, her personality will be forming in the next couple of years. But I have no sense of how I should influence her, relate to her, discipline her. I feel more like her older brother.

"Tell me about your father," said Howard.

My mother divorced my father (for reasons they still argue about) and got custody of me, then three years old, and my two older brothers following a prolonged custody battle. My father lived four blocks away from us on Beacon Hill and we saw him on weekends and occasionally on a weekday. It was always fun. He took us to the zoo, beach, movies or museum. His being fifty years my senior also made him seem more of a grandfather than a father.

The rest of the time, his stand-in was my mother's fourth husband, a Dutchman without tulips. Though this character routinely wore a ten-gallon hat, cowboy boots and striped morning pants with red suspenders, he was no joke to live with. He once kicked to death a drop-leaf table that had dropped his lunch onto the floor.

Adding insult to injury, he liked me best, apparently because he admired the intensity of my hate for him. He was that kind of guy. It took almost thirteen years to get him out of the house, but it was a hollow victory, for my brothers had left home by then and I was about to.

Telling Howard the tragicomedy, dredging up gory details long covered by painkilling time, made me think:

"Boy, you deserve to be confused after all that crap!"
That, I believe, is Howard's intent.

So. I have no role model for fatherhood. I'll have to originate the role.

Susan

June 13

Today in the food store, a wild-eyed woman accosted me with, "Don't you have a stroller? That thing" — she gestured with horror at the frontpack — "is no good for babies."

As if that weren't enough, on the way home a harmless-looking older man approached with a smile, but then said accusingly, "I don't believe your baby can breathe in there."

Where do these sad fanatics, these self-appointed baby experts, come from?

Susan

June 15

After a few visits with Jess in the frontpack, I've decided that the playground depresses me.

How can that be, when the air rings with excited little voices, and there are swings that look like ducks, and a sandbox full of bright pails and shovels?

Sitting on the sidelines, I see other mothers flipping after their children like so many trained seals. They fetch their toys, wipe their noses, kiss their "boo-boos." Some of these women bring bag lunches and thermos bottles and stay all day, knee-deep in sand and kids.

Have they nothing better to do? I hate myself for feeling superior, but their subservience, their stolid presence around the sandbox, annoys me.

Obviously, I haven't made their commitment to full-time child care. I don't think I can.

Michael

June 16
What's all this fuss about changing diapers? The way it is talked about would lead one to believe that changing a diaper was a foul chore, worse than cleaning a fish.

On the contrary, there is a certain pleasure in it. I like swabbing her rosy cheeks, pinning her up in soft cotton. The residue of mother's milk, after all, is pretty tame stuff. And, after all, they are Jessica's dipes.

Perhaps when she becomes a toddler and her diapers are of a wilder nature, I'll change my mind. Meanwhile, I'm enjoying my first experience playing with dolls.

Susan

June 16
When the phone rang, I wasn't expecting it to be a magazine editor offering an assignment. She said she knows I'm busy with Jessica, but the piece has a floating deadline. Best of all, her assistant can do a lot of the research, if I can do the writing.

I don't know when I can do it. Maybe in the wee hours of the morning, after Jess goes to sleep. Or maybe I could write standing up at the kitchen counter, with Jess strapped to my front. (It beats scrubbing floors on my

hands and knees.) Getting the article done will be rough,
but not writing is rougher.

Michael

June 17
Jessica, at three months, is right-handed. Awareness
dawned in that hand, when she learned how to clench
and unclench her fingers, and now it has traveled up her
right arm.

After flailing the arm in front of her face a half-million
times, she finally assumed control. Almost. She still slugs
herself occasionally.

Susan

June 17
"Michael, I don't think we're talking enough," I told him
tonight.

I don't know why it popped out just then. We'd been
having a typical dinner — Jess was fussing, I was trying to
nurse her and eat at the same time, Michael was cutting
my meat for me. For some time now, I've been feeling
that we speak in monosyllables and mumbles, usually
about Jessica or what happened at the office, rarely about
what's going on with us.

Michael's reply floored me. "What's to talk about?" he
said.

Nervously I began rattling on about how other couples
set aside time to catch up with each other. "But you don't
want to leave Jess with a sitter yet," Michael pointed out.

He's right. Joan has been our only sitter so far, and I

don't like to ask her for time on the weekends, when she needs to rest as much as I do.

Still, we can't go on like this.

Susan

June 18

> *Said the kind kangaroo,*
> *"Oh, what shall I do?*
> *If I had a cradle, I'd rock it;*
> *But my baby is small,*
> *so I think after all*
> *I'll carry her round in my pocket."*

The little rhyme my mother used to sing to her children came back to me today. I was surprised, as I crooned to Jess, that I could remember all the words. Surprised, too, that in my own voice, I distinctly heard my mother's.

Michael

June 19
Jessica discovered her toes today, completing her introduction to her body. Well, not quite. She still doesn't know what's under the diaper. That will take a lifetime.

Susan

June 19
I seem to be thinking a lot about my mother lately. Today I got out some old snapshots she'd sent me, of herself and

me when I was a baby. In the fuzzy photos, she is holding me aloft in front of the apartment house where we lived. She is blond and sweet and achingly young in her peasant blouse and wedgie shoes. I am dimpled and moon-faced and look a little like every other baby, and a lot like Jess.

My mother was five years younger than I am, when she had me. Her smile for the photographer was carefully programmed, but what was behind it? Did she feel squeezed, trying to live on my father's teaching salary, in somebody else's house, hundreds of miles from her mother? Was she as surprised as I, to find how much work a new baby is? How much of an intrusion?

"We wanted you so much. You can't believe how excited we were, how many times your father ran to the crib to make sure you were still breathing," my mother wrote me. She doesn't mention that my birth abruptly ended her girlhood and abbreviated her honeymoon.

I wonder if I will gloss over history in the same way for Jessica, when I send her her baby pictures.

Michael

June 20

I was recounting the events of the previous week, telling Howard how much trouble Jessica was giving us, when he interrupted:

"Not Jessica," he said. "It is the decision to have a baby that is giving you trouble."

Absolutely true. What a terrific distinction. It instantly makes me feel easier, because I sometimes sense a strangling conflict in loving her and also wishing she would fall asleep for several weeks. It helps deflect the resentment, attaches the feeling to its proper source, the original decision to have a child, not Jessica.

In the same session with Howard, he caught another bad habit. The conversation was about the way Jessica faithfully ruins our dinners with her screams. "But," I quickly added, "she also makes us laugh with her funny faces."

"She doesn't sound very funny," Howard said, frowning. Then he observed that I frequently use a non sequitur to close off my feelings, ending every gloomy thought on an up note so I don't have to deal with the gloom. The feelings don't flow; I mop them up too quickly, like a spill.

Over and out: the embodiment of my decision to have a baby is crying out for attention.

Susan

June 20

This morning, Jessica was fussing, the kitchen sink was full of dirty dishes, and all I wanted to do was get out of the house — fast. Jess is always quieter in the frontpack, and outside I wouldn't have to look at the crumbs and the twisted sheets and the dirty clothes. But could I leave? No, I had to wait for the diaper man.

As I paced up and down, waiting for Hector, I realized that my whole life seems to be on hold right now. When I'm not held up by a bag of diapers, I'm waiting for Jessica to finish nursing, or for a load of her sleepers to finish churning in the washer, or for Michael to come home and help care for her. (Please, please, come home soon.) Most of all, I feel useless because I've hardly made any progress at all on the magazine piece. After my long time-out from writing, the words refuse to jump onto the page. I squeeze my pen, I jiggle Jess, I pray for a flow of prose, but nothing happens during my stand-up writing stints. Nothing except a lot of scratch-outs and false starts.

When I watch Michael go out the door to his newspaper job these mornings, he looks all buttoned and zippered and ready to go, while I'm left behind in a baggy bathrobe and a messy house. I'm jealous.

Michael

June 21
Today we made home movies. If there is a single thing that makes you feel like a family, it's making a fool of yourselves with a movie camera. We probably looked like the Alfred E. Newmans, carrying on at the Promenade. Under the film direction of our friend Jay, Susie and I acted out the baby rhyme "First comes love, then comes marriage, then comes Michael with a baby carriage." Honest to God. We did it, and without a moment's self-consciousness.

We also took more serious footage: me giving Jess a bath in the kitchen sink, Susie breast-feeding Jess and changing her clothes, and a few cheesecake shots. It was sound film, but Jess didn't utter a peep. How uncharacteristic of her.

Michael

June 22
We are fiercely determined that Jessica will not slow us
down, that she will not change the course of our lives for
the worse. Otherwise, I am sure we would resent her.

So far, it has been impossible to live up to this goal. She
has turned our lives upside down. Exhausted us, separated
us from ourselves, our work, each other, friends, movies,
concerts, trips, money, books . . . I hope this deprived
feeling doesn't last too long. After all, I want her to be a
pure source of pleasure, untainted by ambivalent feelings.
(There it is in black and white. Talk about unreasonable
expectations, whew!)

What is probably most amazing is that I don't have any
ill feelings toward her yet. Perhaps my intense love for her
shields her from these feelings, bounces them into other
parts of my life — which is perhaps why everything else
seems so dreary right now.

Susan

June 23
I've met another mother who reinforces my dislike of the
playground. She is a regular there, her feet planted firmly
in the sandbox as she shifts her seven-month-old daughter
from one safe spot to another. "I don't believe in bottles,"
she tells me stoutly.

"But aren't you worried about the time when you have
to leave her with someone else?" I asked.

"Oh, I don't believe in leaving her with a sitter. At
least, not when she's this young," she replied.

I've felt the same way myself until now, but I'm beginning to rethink the decision. These gung-ho mothers may be able to plant themselves in sandboxes, but I've got to find a better place, a middle ground in which I can be both Jessica's mother and me.

Michael

June 24
As for losses, I mourn spontaneity's more than sleep's. Spontaneity was very important to us because we're such lousy planners. Now we no longer have time to weave romance into our lives, to act quickly on impulses of passion.

In our previous incarnation as a couple, we used to let the weekend roll in, then check the weather and mood, before making plans for dining out, movies, trips. Now, we must think weeks ahead, speculate on future moods, and discuss whether the plan will agree with Jessica.

I can see benefits in becoming thoroughly organized, and I think we may make better use of our free time than we used to, but the priceless loss is the loss in spontaneity between Susie and me. Having a baby has both enriched and sterilized our lives.

Susan

June 26
"Joan, I think I'm going to look for a full-time job," I told my friend today. Not that I was sure I meant it. I just needed to hear myself say it.

At the park with Jess and Andrew, we lolled under a big shade tree. I bit into a pear and tried not to look as scared as I was. I don't know why I've been so miserable lately, but I have. I told Joan about how, each day when Michael goes out the door, I wish I was going, too. To the clean surfaces and set routines of an office, where things are filed and sealed and orderly. Not like home, where laundry baskets overflow, and I forget to each lunch until 3:30. Try as I may, I can't keep the apartment tidy on top of caring for Jessica. And there's never any clearheaded time left for writing. "It's so *hard*," I told Joan, as if she doesn't know. "An outside job is easier. Don't you ever want to go back to editing?"

"Sometimes," she said, lingering over the word. Then her back straightened and she looked decisive. "But not now. No, I've decided I want to be with Andrew during his first year."

She is so strong. I'm not. I'm floundering.

Michael

June 27
After a few sessions with Howard, I felt like putting my experience in perspective. Are other new parents seeking therapy? My reporter's instincts told me there might be a story in it, and there was.

After interviewing several therapists, I found that very few parents seek "preventive" therapy. Everybody has current problems, and only rare types fret about future problems. Where am I? Somewhere in the middle? Howard reassured me that my reasons for starting therapy were valid.

"It is profoundly and sometimes sadly true that children tend to become just what their parents consciously or unconsciously wanted them to become," he said. "For this reason," he added, "knowing oneself well is surely one of the better defenses against 'laying your trip on your child.'"

Most often, parents are in therapy because they can't cope with their children's unrelenting demands, or they disagree on child-rearing practices such as discipline or breast-feeding.

Sometimes, the parents who had a well-balanced marriage before having a baby find their marriage is falling apart under the new stress. Several therapists said the new baby forms a wedge between the parents and, more often than not, the husband becomes the odd man out in the ménage à trois.

In raising children, parents reexperience their own childhood and confront unresolved feelings and failings, Howard said. One anonymous case history he mentioned involved a young father who was deeply disappointed that his six-year-old son had no friends. When the father's feelings were explored, "it became apparent that the real issue was this man's own sense of inadequacy and his own inability to make friendships," said Howard. When the father understood the confusion, he stopped criticizing his son and began helping him make friends, "thereby vicariously experiencing some of the pleasure himself," Howard added.

Nancy Merrill, a family therapist in Chicago, agreed that "we all live through our children. The close identification gives us an opportunity to have both the parent and the childhood we longed for. But it needs a balance," she continued, "and too much identification is unhealthy and puts an enormous pressure on the child."

Nancy added: "But there is no way to avoid making mistakes."

Where are parents most likely to run into trouble? Yvonne Masters, a Manhattan family therapist, said the biggest parental problems are caused by "generational baggage. These are the emotional issues you had difficulty with in the early stages of your development, and these are the very same issues you will have trouble with in raising your own children."

Dr. Martin Cohen, another family therapist in Manhattan, said that many new parents are overwhelmed with an exaggerated sense of responsibility. "They believe the myth that they should be providing everything for the child, taking care of his whole mental, physical, psychological health," Martin said.

Jessica, I realized after doing the interviews, was simply the straw that broke my back. Until she came along, I had been able to stifle my emotional contradictions and frustrations.

But when her birth suddenly turned our lives upside down and deprived me of a great deal of Susie's healing attention, the emotional mud began to rise to the surface.

Jessica made me realize that it was time to get myself thought out, that if I don't resolve my problems, they might become hers. I am so glad I went into therapy now, in the height of the shock of fatherhood, rather than making some quirky adaptation. Believing I needed therapy for Jessica's sake made the decision so much easier.

Thanks, Jess.

Michael

June 28

My first solo excursion with Jessica and her first full day
away from Susie. I was nervous about this first date, but
Jess was cool as a cucumber when we set out.

My mission was to buy a stroller and push her around
for six hours so Susie could work on an article. On the
subway to Manhattan, we did fine, except when I tried to
protect her ears from the drum-cracking noise. She did
not like having her ears tampered with and screamed
louder than the subway-car wheels — a feat, as anyone
who has ridden the city rails knows.

At the baby-furniture store, a gaudy place choked with
cheaply made, bubble-gum-colored junk, Jess was momentarily diverted. But the moment over, she simultaneously became bored, hungry, wet and weepy. I didn't
know which end to start with, but a salesman kindly
steered me toward a changing table and held on to my
squirmy girl's feet.

One step forward, two steps backward. It took almost
an hour to select a stroller. (And when I got home, I was
chagrined to find that my choice did not meet with Man-
agement approval. I had picked a Perego, with an irresist-
ible brown awning, because it looked sturdier than the
more expensive MacLaren. The British vehicle, however,
is about fifteen pounds lighter and more maneuverable.)

Wheeling the little princess around was an adventure
for both of us. We toured all the SoHo galleries rather
compulsively, for as long as I kept her in perpetual motion, she was happy. A pause brought alarm.

At lunch, at a sidewalk café, she took her bottle well
and seemed not to miss the bosom. That was a relief, a

milestone as well. Clearly, I could now take care of her indefinitely by myself. After feeling like a spectator for several months, I have a lot of mothering stored up. I really liked the feeling of being on my own with Jess, and felt that we were getting to know each other better, in a way not possible when Susie is available.

After finishing her milk and crawling over my roast beef sandwich, Jess became fascinated by a dark-haired beauty at the next table. Unblinkingly, she stared until she got a response from the woman, who turned out to be an actress in "As the World Turns." The actress said she also wants a baby, badly. "I've got to find a man first," she said.

I swear, there could be no better way for single men to meet women and get to the heart of things quickly than by pushing a baby around town.

Having pushed Jessica clear across the island twice, I am now a stroller of my former self, but exhilarated that I am finally in on the act.

Susan

July 1

Again we were the "model couple" at the Maternity Center's childbirth class. Only this time we let our battle scars show. We gushed less about the birth experience, grieved more over the crying-jag nights and the disappointing amount of work I've gotten done.

A prospective father who writes Broadway musicals and plans to be a househusband collared me afterward. "I was hoping to be able to rehearse while the baby naps. Think it's possible?" he asked with a nervous smile.

I gave it to him straight. "You know how much writing I've gotten done in four months? Two pages. Both of them lousy."

He gulped, mumbled something about Jessica being beautiful, and hurriedly rejoined his wife.

When we got home, Michael said, "I doubt they'll invite us back."

Michael

July 1

"Saturday nights are still fun," I said, and immediately knew it was a lie. Once again, we were exhibiting ourselves as new parents to a prepared-childbirth class, and I was answering a prospective father's question about how Jessica had affected our sex life.

No, Saturday nights are not always sexy. Far, far from it. It seems nearly impossible to match the time and the mood anymore. Sex has become a lock with a missing combination.

It is very unhealthy. When we do make love, and that colossal tension lifts and is replaced by sweet ease, only then do I remember how important it is for us, together and individually, to make love frequently, preferably on the half hour.

"We should make love whether we feel like it or not," I tell Susie. She languidly agrees, smiles at the absurdity.

But maybe it isn't really that absurd.

Caring for Jessica seems to drain the drive. By the time we have finally coaxed her into her crib, Susie and I are ready for the crib.

Even on good days, when Jessica doesn't take all our

energies, the spark is missing. There is a mysterious inertia about sex hanging over us. We don't feel sexy. It is not on our minds; memories of previous pleasures are cold; feelings that used to propel us from the living room to the bedroom are absent.

Still, under all this false coolness, the need grows as quickly as ever. When it reaches a rapacious level, something finally happens.

No one ever told me that a child works better than a cold shower. I wish I had told that to the class at the Maternity Center.

Michael

July 3

Can't seem to keep that woman, my mother, out of conversations with Howard. She seems to be at the hub of every topic. I start talking about Jessica, Susie, my job or myself and always end up in my mother's lap.

"How do you feel about her?" he asks, again and again.

The woman drives me wild. I love her, I hate her, I love her. She's terrific, talented, funny. She's a menace. One week, after reexperiencing my childhood woes with Howard, I resolve to write the woman off, clean and cool, like a tax depreciation. The next week, I want to share my joy in Jessica with her, a kind of joy only my mother can share. The next week, I resolve to be flexible, to let my emotions breathe. Try to keep a straightforward, uncluttered relationship.

Frightening, isn't it, that the mother-child relationship cuts the pattern for most others?

Susan / East Sullivan, Maine

July 5

If ever three people needed a change, it's Jess, Michael
and me. Maine is like a balm to our frayed New York City
nerves, and Mom is here to help with Jessica while Michael and I go for a sail, or I work on my article.

Today I sat on a big, mossy rock down by the lake and
struggled with the lead paragraphs, which had evaded me
at home. Something about sitting on rock, leaning on
moss, worked like magic, because after a few moments, I
had written a lead that was fine.

Just then, I heard Jessica begin to cry, so I ran back to
the cabin. But my step was light because I felt like a
writer again.

Michael / East Sullivan, Maine

July 6

Grandfatherly reaction to my fatherly activities: shock and
praise.

"Michael, you know just what to do with Jessica," Jerome said, as I went through the consoling routine of offering bottle, checking diaper, and finally frontpacking the
crying doll.

When I've visited my father, he has twice said: "You
certainly know how to whip those diapers on and off."

I don't think either grandfather experienced the intimate
pains and pleasures of caring for his children. It was a
female activity then, like putting on lipstick, and fathers
didn't do it. Now, almost every father I know is equally or
more involved than I am with child care.

Susie, who was almost as naive in these matters as I was a few months ago, does the same chores twenty times as often as I do, but gets no special credit. After all, she's a woman, born with this ability.

Susan / East Sullivan, Maine

July 7

I'm sitting by the lake with Jessica, feeding bread crumbs to the minnows. It's something I've always done on Maine vacations, even when I was a little girl, and it's fun imagining that someday Jess will, too. She squealed when I dipped her toes in the cool water for an instant, but seems to like watching the skittery little fish. Shaded by the brim of her sailor hat, her eyes are as blue as the blueberries we had for breakfast.

I knew it would be fun sharing a favorite place with her, but this trip is really showing me how beautifully she can slip into our life. She's been everywhere with us — to the beach, on lobster picnics, even in the sailboat, where she's enveloped by her bright orange life jacket. Two days ago, when Michael and I hiked the mountain, we took turns toting her in the frontpack. She rode along contentedly, smiling at the pine trees, sniffing the apple-sweet air.

The writing I've been doing, while Mom watches Jess, has restored my sense of balance the way nothing else could. It cheers me to think I might really be able to combine my work with motherhood. Sitting here in God's pocket, it's easy to feel that a good new life has begun.

Michael   /   East Sullivan, Maine

July 7

Like thieves, we stole out of the cabin and crept down to the lake. Cast off the canoe and drifted silently away. This was our maiden voyage, the very first time we were alone, out of sight of Jessica, for four months.

We had come to Maine thinking that Susie's parents would be able to baby-sit a lot, but it was a false hope. Jessica puts up too much of a fuss and we don't feel right about leaving them alone with the screaming meemie. But yesterday, we were prepared to take off with a picnic the second Jess sagged into a deep sleep. The Great Train Robbery wasn't as well planned as this canoe trip.

It was exquisite luxury, those two hours. Paddling around the mountain-rimmed lake. Sitting still, listening to the loons. Not having our little loon to worry about. She was still with us, though. We could feel her presence, much the way a sailor still feels the rolling seas under his feet long after a voyage.

All too soon, we began speculating about Jessica's wakeful state, and reluctantly turned back. As we neared the cabin, we could hear little cries bouncing off the lake. Jessica had discovered the ruse.

Michael

July 8

Snapshot memories of Maine:

(*Snap!*) Jessica taking a bird bath in the pedestal sink.

(*Snap!*) Sitting in her infant seat at the beach, wearing a white derby and the bossy look of a movie director.

(*Snap!*) Crying in the stern of her "Sunny boat," an inflatable plastic raft.

(*Snap!*) Shrieking when her foot slipped into the cold lake water, then frowning angrily at the water. To her, everything is alive.

(*Snap!*) A naked Cupid, on the wrought-iron table, giggling at the camera.

Funny, isn't it, that all my snapshots are of Jessica?

Susan

July 17
I've got the back-to-the-city blues. Where are the loons and the berry fields and the blue mountains over the lake?

Jess is going through some kind of painful passage, too. Every night since we've been home, she's been waking at least once and wanting to nurse. When I mentioned it to Dr. Finkelman, he said, "Yes, lots of mothers home from vacations tell me the same thing."

It's small consolation that lots of babies do it. I've gotten so accustomed to sleeping through the night, this return to broken dreams is all the more shattering. Just when I start feeling smug and comfy, Jess throws me the next curve.

153

Michael

July 18
In talking about my childhood today, Howard commented, "You sound as though you are describing someone else's childhood."

It feels like someone else's childhood.

Did I really grow up in a succession of apartments on Beacon Hill? All filled with stacks of my mother's canvases, furniture on its way to or from one of her rental apartments, and heaps of tools and construction materials needed for their endless renovation.

Had my mother really been married four times? Was my father really an 1896 British gentleman born in Barbados? A warrior of World War I, bwana of an African tobacco farm, overseer of a Cuban sugarcane plantation and husband to J. P. Morgan's niece before marrying my mother? And was she really related to Pocahontas, Chief Justice John Marshall and me?

Did I really live, from my second to my fifteenth year, with her ne'er-do-well Dutchman? That bantamweight with a face full of bone and a billy-goat beard.

"Tell me how you felt then," Howard said, persisting. As I began recalling details, I was shocked that the details hurt, that I was still carrying around childhood sobs and tears.

Long, long ago, I had brushed the emotions aside, unable to cope with them. I never wanted to think about how horrible times in my childhood had affected me. So I lost them as reference points, and never could use them to help explain my dislike for myself, my fear of becoming a father.

I now feel strangely triumphant, powerful, jet-propelled, as I release a childhood's worth of impotent rage. The past is not past, but very present, and I am just getting to know it.

Susan

July 18
Michael said he cried, telling Howard about his childhood. It made me ache to think of Michael being so vulnerable, yet I wasn't surprised at the strength of his reaction.

For as long as I've known Michael, he and his brothers have told knee-slapping stories about their unconventional upbringing on Beacon Hill. Listening to the wild and woolly tales, I pictured them as wolf cubs, sleeping in a huddle around their mother, scrapping with the mates she brought into the den. I slowly learned that beneath the laughter about those days, Michael had other, deeper feelings.

Now he's baring them, and I'm proud of him for being so strong. He seems elated to be finding out so much about himself, grateful to Howard for helping to make it happen, pleased with his own perseverance.

I'm happy for all of us that he's coming to terms with the weights that have been pulling him down.

Michael

July 19
Jessica knows her name! When she discovered that this sound was hers, I don't know exactly. But it is a kick. I say, ''Jessica?'' and she gives an inquiring look with wrinkled brows. The lines of communication are open!

Susan

July 19

In the middle of changing Jessica's diaper, I went down the hall to get a wet washcloth, leaving her on her back in the middle of our bed. When I came back, she was on her tummy.

"Jessica, did you flip yourself over?" I was half delighted, half disappointed that I'd missed her first significant maneuver. "Did you? Did you?"

In reply, she simply rolled her eyes with an ancient sort of wisdom, as if to say, so much for Mum and her need to share the tricks.

Michael

July 20

I'm off again, the proud dad with a month-old Perego and a four-month-old baby. Giving Susie another day for writing and me another day for playing father. It is really a shame that we can't equally share in Jessica's time. Susie sees her too much and I don't see her enough. Isn't that ridiculous? It would be ideal if we both worked outside the house three days a week and stayed home with Jess for four. That way we'd have more than one salary and more quality time with Jessica. Oh, well, things are evening out a bit, now that Jess can be extricated from her mum.

I am now parked on a bench in Central Park, my exultation at caring for Jess alone somewhat tarnished by a scrape with Society. I had planned on spending this steamy morning in the cool, elegant Guggenheim Museum, where Frank Lloyd Wright looped all the picture galleries around a four- or five-story ramp. Tailor-made for strollers, I had thought.

But at the museum, the Nazi behind the ticket counter said, "No strollers!" as though he were rebuffing a dog for using his leg. Why no strollers, I asked, when wheelchairs are allowed on the ramps? "Museum policy," was the dead-end response. I asked to speak with his supervisor, but he, too, was insufferable. Such discrimination! I would think the parents of New York would rise up against such antichild practices.

So, I am out in the heat again. This is one of those fry-an-egg-on-the-pavement days. Jess is melting, but, so far, is in fine form. Swigging from her bottle and gazing around with royal, know-it-all composure. Oops! I take it back: she has just put in orders to march. She is fatigued with this view. So we're off, hopefully to find the magician and jugglers at the other end of the park.

Susan

July 24

The cleaning lady from the islands is a big help, and I feel lucky to have her to do the heavier housework, one half-day a week. But she strains my patience when she starts telling me how to be a mother.

"You think it good to pick her up so?" she asks, when I immediately respond to Jess's cries by handling her. "Why she cry? Put her down in the crib. Let her lie on she stomach. She nurse too much."

Her refrain sends me up the wall, but I don't want to alienate her. So I smile through clenched teeth and offer my standard line: "The baby doctor says I'm doing the right thing."

157

That quiets our lady from the islands for a moment. Until she sees me pick up Jessica again, and the refrain begins anew. "You think it good to pick her up so? Why she cry? Let her lie on she stomach. . . ."

Michael

July 25

Before Jessica was born, Susie never had a cross word for me. Occasionally, and to my instantaneous regret, I have sometimes had one for her. But we never had a protracted argument, and the short ones invariably were in-law inspired and seasonal (deciding which family to spend holidays with is a perennial).

Imagine my disorientation when hard, angry words began tumbling over her lips toward me. On recapturing my senses, I realized that bottom had finally been reached in Susie's deep well of patience and understanding. Jessica has been dipping at this well too long, and the reserve for me is gone.

Spats have entered our life. More often than not, they seem to arise over the way something is said, not the content. "Do you think we could change the menu so I don't gain a pound a week?" I said the other day, sharing my impatience with myself with Susie. Who normally would understand that the message was harmless and would respond in a sensible fashion.

But she no longer has room for my impatience, on top of her own. Told me I'd better do more of the shopping and cooking if I don't like the cuisine. Having a baby, it turns out, is a course in assertiveness training.

Howard believes my so-called harmless messages are in fact the blunt instruments of my anger against Susie.

When complaining about the menu, he said, I am really
bitching about some other problem that I can't bring myself to talk about with her.

I didn't know I was angry at Susie and I didn't think
there was anything I couldn't say to her. Still, what Howard says seems logical, if baffling.

Michael

July 26
After we had waited in line for over an hour to see the
film *La Cage aux Folles*, the assistant manager wouldn't admit us. "No babies allowed," she said, even after we
promised we would leave the theater if Jess woke up and
cried.

What is going on in the world? Everybody seems to
think it is a wonderful thing to have children, but no one
wants to share the responsibility. "People treat kids like
dogs," observed my friend Georgia.

I felt I had to get to the bottom of this stupidity, coming
as it did hard on the heels of my banishment from the
Guggenheim Museum. As luck would have it, I was able
to research attitudes on company time, by doing a consumer story for the Style Page.

I found out that parents are at the mercy of unpubli-
cized, often subjectively enforced antichild rules at theaters, museums, restaurants and other public places. The
rules appear to be based on the belief that all children,
especially infants, cause problems and that all parents are
uncooperative in removing noisy children.

One of the more outrageous policies was at Radio City
Music Hall, which charges everyone $8.50 or $11.00 ad-

mission to its kids' shows, even if an infant or toddler doesn't use a separate seat.

With some exceptions, museums either ban children outright, or exclude them by banning strollers or backpacks. Restaurants rarely have high chairs, some maître d's act irritated when they hear a baby is coming. One said children were admitted only during off-peak hours, in other words, when you're not hungry. Apparently, though I could not verify this, French restaurants are the most intolerant of children, and Chinese, Indian and Italian are the most accommodating.

Susan

July 27

It felt good to be a family today. Jess slept through the night again, so we all awoke feeling sunny and ready for an outing.

On the way to Central Park, Michael snapped some pictures of Jess in front of our local fruit stand. She looked dewy and sweet, squeezed in among the oranges and melons and grapes. Then, on the subway, he took more snaps of her in the squalid car, hemmed in by graffiti and sullen passengers. Sitting in her spiffy new stroller with the sunshade down, she looked wonderfully aloof from it all.

Unfortunately, summer had gotten the best of the park. Broken glass glinted like evil eyes from every patch of grass. Distortion plumed out of a thousand suitcase radios. I suppose the debris and the noise have always been there, but I was more aware of them today. Maybe because I want acres of gentle grass for Jess to roll in. Her beauty makes ugly things uglier to me.

Michael

July 30

Last night I dreamed that Jessica had grown an enormous mane of black hair. I was very disappointed because I had loved her apricot curls. From her birth, I had been rooting for her blond hair and blue eyes to hold fast, because they go so well with her Scandinavian complexion. And, besides, I like blue-eyed blondes.

The dream made me realize I do have strong expectations for Jess. What are the others?

Susan

August 1

"Suse, you've lost so much weight," Joan told me as we strolled our babes to the farmers' market.

"So have you. Just look at that skinny waist!"

We grinned at each other conspiratorially. I was thinking of how far we've come, and maybe Joan was, too. Jess and Andrew are five and six months old now. They're eating solid foods and grabbing toys and growing more responsive each day. And we are nearly our old selves, fitting into our pre-pregnancy clothes, daring to think about our own lives again. Somebody ought to serenade us, give us a key to the city. At the very least.

"Bruce and I looked at a house over the weekend," Joan told me then. "It's in Larchmont."

"Moving?" I didn't want to believe it. "What will I do without you?"

As we wheeled Jess and Andrew past the strawberries and corn and tomatoes, all I could think of was how much I'll miss Joan.

Michael

August 1

This is the summer of anal enticement, according to the *Village Voice*. Every bus ad and billboard has tails wagging and teasing in tight blue jeans. Desire under the skyscrapers.

It is alarming. Women, who have simply been women for years, are becoming visual sex objects for me again. It's an infection. I blame the billboards and television ads for constantly drawing my attention to feminine bumps. But I can't deny it — I find myself gazing with unhealthy, unwelcome, uncontrollable interest. It's sick, I think. They are thoughts, no more, but they make me feel disloyal, unfaithful, inhuman, wretched and a few other things. Is it my fault or Calvin Klein's? Is this the beginning of the end of my marriage? How could this be happening?

I admit the dilemma to Howard, and ask: Why do I want something I know I absolutely do not want? Why am I torturing myself?

"When are your feelings strongest?" he asks. When everything is blahing along, I answer. When I'm bogged down at work, exhausted at home, or when Susie's away for the weekend.

"What is causing it?" I ask. Howard suggests I am not looking for sex, but for that aggressive, powerful feeling that would accompany making a pickup. To compensate for my pent-up sexual frustration at home. And it has to do with feeling abandoned by Susie, too.

Previously, in those normal times before baby, Susie and I didn't talk about sex; we didn't have to. There were plenty of naturally occurring romantic interludes. Now there are none and I need to adapt to the new situation by being more open and earthy, less neurotically shy.

Good God! I thought on the way home. I got caught in that cliché about new parents being pushed apart by baby and the father getting depressed or worse. It happened and I didn't even know it.

I went into Altman's and bought Susie a fire-engine-red negligee.

Susan

August 2

It was alarming when Michael blurted out last night that he notices other women more now. I heard a siren go off in my head. Is this the first sign of trouble for us?

I really don't think so. I tell myself that as long as his interest doesn't go past looking, I can understand his feelings, rationalize them, even.

I haven't exactly been looking like Catherine Deneuve for a long time now. I can never find the time to get my hair done. I've only recently lost my new-mother lumpiness.

I haven't been acting like Catherine, either. My body feels overused, after being handled by Jessica all day. By night, I'm too tired and bruised to care about any more touching. So, while Michael feels fairly obsessed by sex, I can't bear to think of it at all. Most nights, it is absolutely the farthest thing from my mind.

It's funny, but more than Michael, I seem to be able to put these changes into perspective. I know this awkward time won't last forever. I suspect that other couples with new babies experience it, too.

In a stubborn sort of way, I still feel very secure about Michael's love for me, and about how good we are for each other.

∽*163*

Michael

August 3
Jessica has gotten very grabby all of a sudden. She wants to touch the world. This morning the little crab was sitting peacefully in my lap one second and the next, she had grabbed my cup of steaming hot coffee. She managed to scorch her hand and my leg.

A waterfall of tears, a stunned look of betrayal.

She is just beginning to learn how insensitive the world is. "It's not easy being a baby," Susie says, trying to comfort the crab.

Susan

August 4
My artist friend, whose name also is Susan, asked me on a walk today if I was getting much writing done. I told her I've finally finished my first assignment, but the effort flattened me. I don't know when I'll have the energy to tackle another.

"How about weekends? Does Michael help?" she asked.

"Well, usually he wants to run around, so we run around with him," I heard myself say, with a grudging undertone that I hadn't realized was there.

"That's all right," she said, trying to smooth my hackles.

Sometimes it is. Our outing to Central Park was a great success, even with the park in shoddy shape. But sometimes we have a problem because Michael likes to pretend that nothing has changed, that we can run around as much as we did before Jessica. I get very tired, repacking the diaper bag and keeping up the pace on some of these marathon weekends. I feel ambivalent about wanting to spend time as a family, yet needing more time for myself.

I don't like being the heavy, reminding him that everything is different now. I certainly don't like admitting that life is less than a bowl of Godiva chocolates. It seems so boring to want to stay home on weekends. But after a week of caring for Jessica, I'd often just like to slip her to Michael and slide into a forty-eight-hour bubble bath.

Michael

August 8
Therapy thought: Why does Mother get all the blame? And Father get off scot-free? Is it because she did all the child care, was around the children all the time, influenced them the most — and so was liable to make more mistakes? Be held more responsible?

While Father played a safer game, giving gifts, friendship and a few stern words. Strong, strange mother; absent, easygoing father = hot and cold feelings about her; warm, unqualified acceptance of him. Nobody said life is fair.

Susan

August 12
It was my turn to baby-sit for Joan, and I was on Atlantic Avenue — a wide street full of dusty shops — with Andrew in the stroller and Jessica in the frontpack. Andrew began to wail and wail. I looked around helplessly, saw

two painted ladies in a doorway, and decided I had to ask them for help.

"Oooh, I'd love to," said the one with pink streaks in her hair. "I never get to hold a baby."

Just then a boyfriend appeared, and an argument flared. Pink Streaks showed her teeth as she spat out angry words, kicked her boots into the pavement.

"It'll be all right, it'll be cool," her friend kept saying, but I couldn't take any chances. Not with two babies caught in the middle.

Hastily I tossed Andrew into the frontpack, retrieved Jess from the tigress's grasp, and rolled the stroller double-time up the avenue.

"It could only happen to a big-city mom," I told Michael at dinner, and we both laughed at the funny side of my predicament. But I think what I'll remember most about today is the slow, sad way that Streaks said, "I never get to hold a baby."

Michael

August 13

Children have the same status as Chihuahuas. Perfect strangers walk up to Jessica on the street and start fondling her apricot curls.

Naturally, Jessica cringes in disgust at this intimacy. Sometimes, she lets out a yelp of indignation, roughly translated as: "Please, I deserve respect! Even if I am incontinent and incommunicado!"

Strangers are taken aback, and Susie or I explain that it takes Jess a while to warm up to people, to determine if their intentions are honorable and if they will play the game her way.

Her uncle Peter jokes that Jessica responds only to "authorized handlers," in other words, her trained slaves, Susie and me.

Michael

August 15
Having a baby just before summer was supposed to be a good idea.

Whoever coined this cliché obviously had an insulated attic or lived outside the frying pan of New York City. When I came home from work today, Susie and Jess looked as though they had been swimming in their clothes. I ripped off mine before they got drenched and started emptying cans of beer. Even Jess took a sip.

Susan

August 18
After a long absence, I went back to the playground today, and saw it with new eyes.

The mothers I met around the sandbox were lively, interesting women whose minds haven't turned to mud pies. One is writing a source book for new parents. Another makes toys from spools and other homey materials. A third belongs to a parents' exercise group that I might like to join. They related to their children in creative ways, too — asking them questions, thinking up games, being much more than sandbox groupies.

I'd never really talked to any of them before. I see now that I've been missing something.

Michael

August 18

"Jessica, in 1996 when you're sweet sixteen, you can bring your dates home for double dates with your mom and dad. We can sit around the fire and make popcorn," I told her this evening. Naturally, she cried.

It will be strange, watching this little bundle stretch into a nymph with a trail of boyfriends. I wonder how I will feel when she does have dates. Will I be jealous, competitive, worried about her being hurt by some cruel adolescent? Or will I be a rational, understanding third party?

I see that Jessica will be introducing me to new emotions for the rest of my life. I hope I will like them.

Michael

August 22

Therapy is an intellectual whip. Held over my head, it forces me to dwell on unpleasant topics. The more unpleasant the topic, the more important it must be to talk about, Howard claims.

Today, he prompted me to talk about my self-image. Not a fun subject.

I have been feeling better about myself ever since I met Susie, an ego booster without equal in the universe, I tell him. The bad stuff is past, over with. Let's talk about something else, I suggest.

"Nothing is past," Howard says, drearily. Emotional luggage is with us forever, but it can be sorted, cleaned, understood, and rendered less painful, he adds.

Okay. There are good reasons for me to dislike myself. "A late bloomer" were the kindest words any teacher had for me. My two older brothers, who knew everything, used crueler expressions. For twenty-seven years I bumped around, unhappily going nowhere.

I was a failure for so long it is hard getting used to my recent success, I tell Howard. But as he sees it, I so successfully programmed myself for failure that I can't enjoy victory.

It resonates.

Coincidentally, I read that Dr. Shepard Kellam at the University of Chicago has linked failure in the first grade to later psychological problems. "We have to stop failing children in the first grade and stop failing to help them master tasks," he said. I hope my first-grade teacher is listening. I'll make sure Jessie's does.

Michael

August 23

We're figuring it out, slowly but surely. The pool club in Manhattan, we discovered, is a great place to take Jessica on these hot summer weekends when we can't get out of the city.

She likes dipping her feet in the water and watching the swimmers. We would like to teach her to swim, but the club doesn't allow diapered children in the pool. (At the Y, though, there are swimming classes for babies and they have no qualms about babies tinkling in the pool; all the young kids do it anyway, they say, and the filtration system can handle it.)

Our routine: Susie or I, and sometimes my brother Peter, carries Jess around the pool while the others swim. It is refreshing and everybody has a good time.

If we ever have another baby, we will know just what to do. Or as Jim, my friend at work, said: "For the first baby, you sterilize the bottles; for the second baby, you wash the bottles; for the third baby, you just rinse the bottles." But now, Jessica is beginning to feel like our second baby.

Susan

August 26
Jessica's first painting exhibition was a biggie — the Picasso show at the Museum of Modern Art. When Susan called to say she had tickets, I wavered about how Jess would weather the slow, snaky lines on a hot day. But now I'm really glad I took the chance, because Jess was a peach. She soon settled down to a nap in the frontpack, while Susan and I drifted past the portraits of sad-eyed women, the wooden toys carved for the Picasso children, the heroic canvases of christenings and clowns and war. A radio news reporter, gathering interviews on his tape recorder, asked me, "How does your baby like the show?" I told him that Jess was wowed by all the earthy colors and undulating shapes, until it was time for her to snooze.

Afterward, we sat in the sculpture-filled garden while Jessica nursed and Susan watched. "I don't think I want to have children," Susan said suddenly.

That surprised me. Susan and I had never discussed it before, so I wasn't sure how she felt. But she's always shown a wild enthusiasm for Jess. The collage she made for us when Jess was born was the best of all the baby cards, a merry concoction of cupids, blossoms and bluebirds. But I kept quiet as she continued: "You can sit at the typewriter with Jessica in the frontpack. But I couldn't paint holding a baby. It just wouldn't work."

I admire Susan's single-mindedness. Knowing what I now know about the demands of child care, I can only agree with her conclusion that her work would suffer if she had a baby.

I still don't know how much Jess will affect my work. But sitting in the garden at that moment, watching Jess's head bob at my breast, I felt my own decision reaffirmed. "All I know," I told Susan, "is that I'll never create anything more beautiful than she is."

Michael

August 27

I've just heard it is passé to have family photos on one's desk at work. That is the kind of drivel you hear in New York, where people are always looking for easy ways to outclass one another.

By this standard, I am très passé: the wall behind my desk is picture-to-picture family. Blowups of Susie pressing Jessica's cheek to hers; of sister Paula, brown and golden, and Jessica, pink and white, at a Virginia beach; of nude Jessica, with cheek in fist in a ridiculous version of Rodin's *Thinker*.

The wall is a window for daydreaming. Today, I added a new picture to the gallery and unabashedly drew my colleagues' attention to it. Modesty is a pointless drag.

Michael

August 28

Jessica hasn't crawled yet, hasn't gotten her teeth yet, hasn't said a word yet. So what? Exactly, but seeing other babies about her age doing these things makes me want to see my little chunk do some tricks, too.

Is this the first sign of Little League Syndrome?

Michael

August 30

At the Bronx Zoological Gardens, with the yaks, flamingos and Jessica. For four years Susie lobbied unsuccessfully for a trip to the zoo, but now, she has an ally. Jessica was demanding that we go somewhere, do something, *immediately*. Summer in the city. We had done the parks and the Staten Island ferry and the swimming pool umpteen times. The zoo, despite the heat and the long subway trip to get there, sounded feasible.

Jessica looked at the wild animals with the same interest she has in people on the subways. This interest is characterized by long, hard looks with little or no comment. The gorillas, snakes and elephants are, I suppose, just more strangers for her to absorb.

Only the tiger with his wild eyes scared her. Jessica must have understood his hungry look, for she let out a yelp and held my shoulder tight.

It was fun. Even the long subway ride wasn't as bad as I expected. In previous years, the mere thought of an hour in the subway worked up enough inertia to kill an excursion. Jessica, however, devours inertia.

Michael

September 1

Newborns cry between one and four hours a day, according to one baby book, so why can't I just sit back and accept it? Because it is a torturous sound, one that bypasses all rationalization.

Howard, my wise man, says that Jessica's crying may be evoking unconscious memories of my own childhood. That her crying makes the child in me cry, unleashing feelings of unfulfilled needs. She is touching wounds that have never healed. Howard wants me to talk about these wounds, as far back as I can remember.

Wound One: I am a toddler, between three and five years old. My mother and two older brothers walked much faster than I could and frequently left me far in their wake. I found this lonely and disconcerting. One summer morning, I was trailing behind them as they rushed down Beacon Hill. I screamed at them to wait for me. They didn't, and I was consumed with fury.

"Did your mother ever respond to your anger?" Howard asked.

"No, I don't think so. It never seemed to bother her."

"Do you know how strange that is?" he said. "If someone as important to you as your mother acts as though your feelings do not matter, you might also begin to think your feelings didn't matter. That they were worthless, that you were worthless," he said, quietly. "Does this have any resonance, does this sound right to you?" he asked.

Yes, it does.

He said I avoid telling people about my needs, assuming that they, like my mother, wouldn't find them worthy of addressing. My emotions then get bottled up until the bottle cracks and, suddenly, I find myself mad as hell at my mother or brothers.

I am scared that, someday, I might vent one of these tempers on Susie or Jessica. But now I know whence fury came. Next I must find out if that helps.

Little does Jessica know that her tears are carrying me through an examination of my whole emotional life.

Michael

September 7

Nobody gives advice like mothers; it flows with the milk. They have such absolute confidence that they are right. It is well-meaning advice — they want to save you some misery they had. The only hitch, as far as I can see, is that each little bundle of trouble has many unique problems, which require solution by trial and error, error and error.

"Don't jiggle Jessica too much or she'll grow up fidgety," Mother Clara said, with a straight face. (I looked at her son Dick, wondering if he is the way he is today because of too many bounces on his mom's knee. Although he doesn't actually shake, he is a drifting, impulsive sort.)

Another mother nipped at our heels for ten minutes, insisting that newborn Jessica *needed* solid food. And she was astonished to hear of Susie's open-ended nursing plan. "What? Let the baby wean *you?*" she asked.

I became more tolerant of these sermons after hearing Susie preach to a mother with a younger baby about the value of bottle-feeding. ("Don't give up the bottle completely, or else the baby won't take it later on. I had a real hard time with Jess," she said.)

Susan

September 8

I was sitting in the playground with Jess when a small woman, about my mother's age, approached with a smile. She had an easy manner and Kewpie-doll eyes, saucy and round. After some small talk, she stunned me by asking, "Are you interested in getting a baby-sitter?"

What startled me was her intuition. Is it so obvious that I need help? Or is she just a good businesswoman, with a sharp eye for six-month-olds?

No matter. My September song to Michael has been, "I'm going back to work half-days this fall." He's been encouraging me to do it. But until today, I'd done nothing to realize the scheme.

Tonight I called the woman's references. They raved and raved. "Ann is the best," said one Brooklyn Heights mother. "She'll treat your daughter like her own grand-daughter," said another.

That's what I need, someone kind and caring who will help reduce the feelings of guilt that are already perking. I think I can lick the guilt if I know Jess's caregiver is a loving person.

Tonight my head feels light as a bubble. I'm going back to work.

Michael

September 9

I got angry with my mother today on the telephone. Her response: "I'd like to hack the head off that therapist of yours."

I told Howard he had better cover his neck if approached by an elderly lady with banana-colored hair and a fiendish look. He laughed, nervously.

Susan

September 9

Nan visited today. She's a middle-aged friend whose situation is far different from mine.

Her husband died suddenly last year. Her grown children's lives have gone haywire. Her daughter is a sixties burnout. Her son vacillates between joining the revolution in Central America or a communal farm in Tennessee. Nan's whole body shrinks when she speaks of her children, in half whispers.

I'm glad that she has her work as a free-lance photographer, poorly paid though she may be. Over mugs of cider, she told me about a small newspaper that pays her a few dollars for her pictures. Her face glowed as she showed me the clippings of her published work, her fingers stroking the bits of paper in their plastic sleeves.

Spending time with her made me wonder: What will I do, if someday Jessica chooses a life I can't approve of? Will I whisper her name, try to lose myself in work?

The longer I'm a parent, the more I see it as a precarious existence.

Michael

September 10

Jessica spoke her first nonsense syllable that made sense: "Da da, da da!"

She said this very emphatically, without equivocation or
prodding, to her big toe. But no matter, I was delighted
and Susie, appalled. I had won the race that had become
a competition only after I won it.

Jessica likes the feel of this sound and she beats it like a
drum. "Da-da-da-da *da da!!*" When she sees something
she really likes, she says, *"Da!"* Imperiously demanding it.

It's funny. I used to cringe at the sound of "daddy" and
was determined that no child of mine, if there were one,
would refer to me with that Kool-Aid noise.

"The baby can call me Michael, Uncle Herbert or anything but Daddy," I told Susie when she was pregnant.
My bride, who has twice as much strict German blood in
her veins as Polish, was horrified. Children have to have
respect for adults, she said; they can't call their parents by
their first names.

Today, I told Susie I liked the way Jess said "Da da."
"I'm glad you're off that first-name kick," she replied.

Susan

September 11

Took a walk with Mai. She's another new mother who
lives here in the neighborhood. The first time I met her,
she rolled her stroller up to my toes, smiled, and said,
"Aren't you glad your baby is a girl?"

She wasn't smiling today. She said she's been going
through a terrible depression. It began when her year-old
Kate fell down the stairs. Mai said she began to ask herself
whether it was her fault, and whether she deserved to
have a child at all.

As she spoke, I had to look away, embarrassed, because
I've judged her a little harshly sometimes myself. Every

time I see Kate at the playground, she seems to have a cold, or a bump from a fall. I've wondered if Mai isn't a little careless, letting her daughter tear around their brownstone home without enough supervision.

Why can't I be more generous? Hearing the pain in Mai's voice made me realize how wrong I was. In my way, I've been just as judgmental as the harpies who swoop down on me for using the frontpack.

After I let Mai talk about her guilt feelings, I talked about my own. I told her about how I've felt a pang these first days, getting Jess ready for her sitter. How little Jess seems, to be separated from me. And yet how much I need the space.

Dismissing guilt as a senseless, negative emotion is easy when it's someone else's guilt. When it's my own, I'm stuck with it.

Michael

September 13
Finally, we rented a film projector to view our home movies. They are terrific! I can't believe how much Jessica has already changed in this short time. She looked so tiny and square and bald.

Mr. Kodak, I see, is going to make a killing on us.

Susan

September 15
Went back to the office where I kicked off my New York career, and was reassured to see everything looking as funky as ever.

The publisher's desk was lost in a snowbank of letters, memos, and desperate messages from his production manager. The plaque on the wall, bestowing the Pope's blessing, hung at a rakish angle. The sofa, unfit for a sit-down, was crammed end to end with stacks of old magazines that the small, family-owned company has churned out over the years. Car books. Quilt books. Diet books. UFO books. Any old kind of book that might earn a buck. "I'm going to get this place cleaned up this week," the publisher told me solemnly. As he has for the five years I've known him.

He's still surrounded by the same pleasantly offbeat group of employees. The Haitian woman with the incomprehensible accent, who handles all phone transactions for the front office. A slick-haired Indian whose only known responsibility is changing the light bulbs. A dusky Panamanian who puffs cigars big as bananas and dispenses Caribbean charm along with the paychecks. No chic secretaries with chignons, or trendy art directors in thigh-high boots, for Mr. L.

In his office, he said he wants me to do some writing for his magazines. "But don't leave that baby of yours with a sitter, whatever you do. I don't believe in that," he told me sternly.

I smiled, said nothing. I love Mr. L. But like most people, he imagines that I can do the impossible, type with my big toe while I conduct a phone interview with one hand and jounce Jessica in the other.

Michael

September 16
She's two foot two, her eyes are blue. My gal weighs in at seventeen pounds, four ounces. Last week she was six

months old. She still has this fetish about being held up-right and kept in constant motion. With her strapped on my chest, I walked a figure-eight pattern, looping through the living room and bedroom, for over two hours last night. Whenever I tried to sneak a rest on the sofa, she would immediately stir and begin to cry.

"Please stay asleep," I whispered lovingly, through clenched teeth. We need one of those stand-up armchairs, the kind used in Hollywood for actors who can't bend in their costumes.

Susan

September 17
Housework is a problem.

It always has been, with both of us working, but now it's getting worse. Caring for Jessica consumes time and energy that I once tossed into homemaking. These days, with the house looking mostly like an unmade bed, I feel dissatisfaction gnawing at me in a ratty sort of way.

I've begun to see that there isn't much of a division of labor in our house. I make the plane reservations, pick up the dirty socks, thaw the chicken, write the thank-you notes. When Michael loads the dishwasher or picks up some groceries, I feel compelled to thank him. The impli-cation is that he is helping me with work that is mine, not sharing responsibility that is ours together.

But how can I blame him for this sorry state of affairs, when I helped put it in motion? Looped on love, I spent our first days together in a frenzy of domesticity, simmer-ing stews and sauces, stitching up curtains for our big, bare windows.

No, it isn't completely his fault that we're stuck with a stereotypical domestic situation. I've nursed it along, with my fantasies of hot muffins on cold mornings, crisp sheets, homemade costumes on Halloween. All the cozy touches that my mother provided for me. Sometimes, I still daydream about being Supermom. But in wide-awake moments, I realize that I desperately need a Superdad, just to keep the house livable.

I hear variations on the theme from friends. "It's terrible, but cooking is the one thing he just won't do," says one, a gourmet cook who still tries to knead bread with one hand while jiggling her baby with the other. "He can't stand to put his hands in dishwater," says another friend with two small children, who works nights in a supermarket. That's how she explains the fact that when she staggers home from her job around midnight, there's still a sinkful of dirty dishes for her to do.

Some of these guys are great at caring for their kids, thanks to prepared-childbirth classes and their own desire to get involved, so the picture is not entirely black. Michael assumes more of Jessica's care every day. Some things have changed for the better.

But more things have to, if I'm going to feel good about our home. Forget about fancy desserts and homemade Halloween costumes; I'd just like to walk across the living-room floor without tripping. Michael's got to help me keep from falling.

Michael

September 17
I like the idea of Susie breast-feeding Jessica for as long as they both like it. Sometimes, when Susie says she would

like to reclaim her breasts, I think, "Oh, well, too bad. It would have been nice if she could have let Jess wean her."

But lately, the thought has occurred to me that I, too, would like to have Susie's body back. It has been on loan for a long time. And, I must admit, it would be nice if her breasts regained some of the mysterious allure that's been lost during the months they've served as milk bottles.

A while ago, when I was telling Howard the trauma our sex life was suffering, he brought up the subject of breast-feeding. He said that, for a variety of reasons, including possible hormonal changes, women generally feel sexier after they have stopped breast-feeding.

An interesting thought. I don't want to push Jess aside, but now I look forward to the day when she'll lose her taste for hot milk.

Michael / Boston

September 20

"Why don't you put Jessica to bed and let her sleep?" my father asks. A straightforward question that makes my eyeballs pop. I explain that it is not for our pleasure that we constantly nurse and entertain Jessica, that her being fussy does not mean she is tired enough to sleep. If we put her to bed, her cries would crack the crystal in his house. Probably his windows, too.

The current theory is that you don't let babies cry and cry and cry. It is bad for them to cry themselves to sleep. They are terrified and feel helpless, powerless, that their cries bring no response.

"'You can't spoil a baby for the first year' — that is the

rule we are living by," I said. It is a tough rule, but certainly no tougher than it would be to hear her wailing in her crib for an hour.

My father shakes his head dubiously. He doesn't believe in "newfangled theories." Maybe he is right. We'll never know.

Susan

September 22

Grump, grump, grump. Sometimes I feel as if I can't stop complaining.

I tell myself that I should be in seventh heaven, now that writing is in my life again. When Jessica comes back to me in the early afternoons, I feel so refreshed, so eager to see her and kiss the soft hollow at the back of her neck. At those times I feel I've solved the problem of how to combine motherhood and meaningful work. That elusive state that so many women seek, that the women's magazines always dub "the best of both worlds," seems to be mine, all mine.

Still, I find lumps in my oatmeal. Today, for example, when I tried to compile a list of story ideas for editors, I realized that I have no ideas. I think it's because I've barely read a word in over six months. Newspapers, magazines, new books, float into the house, and I get a tantalizing glimpse of their covers. But never do I get to read them.

It's incredible to realize that I can be Michael's wife and Jessica's mother and a part-time writer, but there may not be time for anything else. Certainly not for a slow read in an easy chair.

Michael

September 22
"When did Billy get his tooth?"
"Do you like the Perego stroller?"
"A and D ointment smells better than Desitin."
Baby talk, baby talk. When we get together with friends who have a baby, the conversation dwells on size two. Not that I can't spend ten minutes swapping diaper-rash stories. It is enjoyable to share this new universe with friends. But sometimes, it seems that we are being consumed by it.

Michael

September 23
"I want to know, *right now*, what *else* are we going to need? What else could we possibly need?" I said, after Dale and Rick sprang the news on me.
Jessica, they said, will soon need another crib, one with high sides to contain her. Her "old" wooden crib, like the first stage of a rocket, is now useless. It makes perfect sense.
But it comes at a time when I had just thought we were fully equipped. We've got jolly jumpers coming out of the closet, an elaborate swing, musical mobiles, a portable crib she has never used, a wicker crib she has rarely used, a playpen, a walker, lightweight stroller, heavyweight stroller, backpack, frontpack, diaper bags and pail, toy hampers and toys everywhere. Our apartment looks like a "chip and dent" sale at F.A.O. Schwarz. But Rick, who has two children and ought to know, said our collection has just begun.

With that, I decided I no longer want to know everything we are going to need. A little startle at a time, please.

Michael

September 24
Susie, bouncing Jess on her knees, sings:

> *''Ride a cockhorse*
> *To Banbury Cross*
> *To see a fine lady*
> *Upon a white horse.*
> *Rings on her fingers and*
> *Bells on her toes,*
> *SHE SHALL HAVE MUSIC*
> *WHEREVER SHE GOES!*
> *SHE SHALL HAVE MUSIC*
> *WHEREVER SHE GOES!!!''*

At the finale, when Susie's knees are really pumping, an expression of the purest delight bursts into Jessica's eyes and she giggles velvety gutturals, punctuated with wind-chime shrieks. Then it's over. Faster than a finger-snap, Jess has regained her composure and is looking for the next moment's pleasure.

"Do it again," I plead, a junkie for baby laughs. Susie sings and bounces again, and again Jess's toothless mouth widens into a nearly perfect rectangle of joy. Such a square kid.

One of these moments provides enough emotional fuel to get through at least one fractured mealtime. It is also the kind of memory that will outlive all other dreary ones.

Susan

September 25

Last night as I was sleeping, Jessica choked softly in her crib. I was on my feet instantly and running to her side.

I found her vomiting quietly, her body limp. The sight terrified me. She's been so impeccably healthy all these months, I've been lulled into feeling that my milk keeps her safe from all evil. I trembled as I sponged her, changed her sleepers, tried to comfort her. Everything seems so much worse in the night. After she went back to sleep, I tossed and worried until light hit the windows.

This morning when I saw that Jess was pink and sound and smiling again, I sagged with relief. An overnight rebound. That's my baby!

Tonight poor Michael seems to have been bitten by the same bug. He's been lying around with a hangdog look, holding his stomach and moaning, "How did Jessica ever come through it so well?"

Michael

September 28

Luckily, Susie never sleeps. Some part of her brain is always plugged in, ready to receive signals from baby Jess. She heard "something funny" the other night and found Jessica gagging in a puddle of her own sickness. Jessica had the flu.

But she had it for only a few hours, it seemed. Then Susie carried it around for a day before giving it to me. Now, either females are tougher than males, which is beyond belief, or else the flu bugs had grown meaner by the time they tackled me. Jessica's three-hour flu knocked me out for thirty-six.

Susan

September 29
Something very good is happening. Michael seems to have more energy for us since he went into therapy.

It's as if talking to Howard, tracing his conflicts to their roots, has blown the lid off Michael's internal pressure cooker. None of the steam is wasted, either.

Most nights now, after dinner, Michael loads the dishwasher, then draws a tub and takes a long bath with Jessica. While they bob around in a flotilla of plastic boats, I have a little time alone to sip a second cup of coffee and sometimes even read a bit of the newspaper.

It's a small chunk of time compared to the rest of the day, but it comes when my patience and energy are ebbing. A cup of coffee never tasted better.

It's taken time for me to tell Michael about my needs, and for him to tell me about his. But I think we're coming together, finding out what it takes to be a family.

Michael

September 29
Suggested government issue for every new parent:

- Several sets of wail-absorbing earplugs
- Rose-colored glasses to obfuscate litter
- Sensory deprivation tank for peace and quiet

- Computer dating service to locate foster grandparents, marriage counselors, therapists
- Organic, time-release tranquilizers
- Emergency wet-nurse service
- Two-year supply of megavitamins
- Toll-free Hot Line for a digest of current baby-care theory
- Toll-free Scream Line with operators who accept screams
- Two hundred rolls of Kodachrome movie and slide film

Michael

September 30
Jessica's vocabulary is growing geometrically. She now says *ma!*, *cha!* and *deedle deedle dee*. *Cha!* is by far her favorite. It has replaced *da!* as her exclamatory comment. And *ma!* is often a one-word complaint.

Susan

October 1
The phone rang early. It was Fran, wanting to know if I'd seen the *Daily News*. "They've got a big article on Angela Ambrosia," she said, sounding more subdued than usual. "Her funeral is today."

No no no no no.

When I got back to the breakfast table, everything was normal. Michael was spooning cereal into Jess's mouth, and complaining when it spattered his tie. "Angela's dead," I said. "I always meant to take Jessica to see her. Angela loved babies so much." My face fell apart.

Michael looked down at his plate and didn't say anything. I think he understood how desolate I felt.

Michael

October 2

I've heard it said that babies cry one way when they have wet diapers, another way when they're tired, another way when hungry. Jessica hasn't heard this story. She cries one way, with increasing volume, for every occasion.

And if dirt in the dipe did bother her, one would never know it from the way she frets and fumes when she is being changed. Squirm, kick, twist and slide; diapering an octopus would be easier. Apparently, she finds it an indelicate procedure, one impinging on her dignity. I would feel the same way — but really, isn't she supposed to be a seven-month-old baby who doesn't know any better?

And when the struggle is over, she acts triumphant, as though she has won out. Well, one of the reasons I wanted a baby girl was to observe this strange sex from the ground up. As yet, Jessica remains a mystery. So much for science.

Michael

October 6

It is dinnertime. Jessica, the pride, joy and curse of the Lapinski-Hinds household, has just finished rubbing a chicken puree into her hair. During the chicken shampoo, some got in her eyes, causing her to become very angry with the chicken and its servers. The dinner bowl is tossed on the floor with a great flourish.

We finally wised up and now lay a drop cloth under her majesty. She has such a discriminating palate. If she tires of potato in the middle of a bite, *pit-touie!* out she spits it. No sense wasting her taste buds, even for a second.

So eccentric, so set in her ways and not a year old yet. It is a pity, in a way, that this wild thing must be tamed.

Susan

October 15

For months I've looked forward to the reunion of our pre-pared-childbirth class, complete with the babies we produced. Tonight was worth the wait.

As each couple walked through the door of the Maternity Center, Michael and I exclaimed at the sight of their progeny. Jim and Linda had always said they expected a girl, and there was Arianna, with Jim's nose and Linda's eyes and enough lace ruffles to convince anyone of her femininity. Valerie and Robert's Jeremiah was a doe-eyed dandy; Linda and Kevin's Joshua, a budding strong man with a barrel chest and a pair of wild cowlicks. Each baby was winning and wonderful in a different way.

When it was time to eat, Jess and the other babies tumbled around together on rubber mats on the floor, while we adults shared the food we'd brought, quiche and salad and cake and wine. And of course we shared baby news, asking each other, "Are you still nursing?" and "Is he standing yet?" and "Did you ever think it would be so much work?" Nobody had. We kept telling each other how beautiful our babies are, and how we must keep in touch with each other.

Maybe we will. Probably we won't. Still, there's a special bond with these couples who learned how to huff and puff and push out a baby at the same time we did.

Michael

October 18
"Nothing is as sad to me as seeing parents wait for a child to exhaust himself enough to ask for bed," says Dr. T. Berry Brazelton. I agree. It is a bum experience for everyone, but is bedtime really the parents' decision, as he suggests?

Jess still screams unbearably when put to bed, as though we are burying her alive. Her cries are much worse than at any other time. Being alone in her crib seems to terrify her. Dr. Brazelton may be right, but we can't handle it.

Susan

October 23
Michael brought home a clutch of new toys for Jess tonight. One is a blue plastic telephone with hippos dancing around the dial. Another is a jack-in-the-box with a bear that swivels into view, after the box plays a jangly version of "The Bear Went over the Mountain."

The telephone made Jess's lower lip quiver, and the bear's sudden appearance evoked howls of anger. Michael was crestfallen that his gifts didn't go over better.

I sort of expected it. Jess is a little young for such sophisticated toys. She likes her felt bunny and her rubber starfish and her animal key ring. But when she tires of them, as she does quickly, she simply drops them out of sight. There is a wonderful economy to her needs.

What she needs, most of all, is closeness. Today I pared vegetables while she sat in her infant seat on the counter. She watched the slicing and paring warily for a few moments, then fussed to be held. When I picked her up again, her whole body snuggled into mine, and she began to knot her fingers into my hair.

Of all her toys, I am her favorite.

Michael

October 30

When did Jessica start communicating? It crept up so slowly, no milestone comes to mind, just pebbles. For a few weeks she has been shaking her head from side to side, mimicking our "no." Occasionally, she seemed to understand that it means "no"; the rest of the time, she just liked the emphatic feeling of the movement.

Last night at dinner, though, she suddenly seemed to appreciate the awesome power of "no." A spoonful of peas was heading her way and she shook her head violently. The peas were withdrawn and Jessica, visibly surprised, gave a self-satisfied smile, the kind she tries to hold back by sucking in her lips. "Ahah!" she seemed to be thinking, "I am gaining better control of my slaves! All I have to do is shake my head to operate them."

Same with pointing. She has been pointing with her index fingers forever. Usually accompanied by sound effects and usually done, it seemed, to say: "Hey! Look what I'm looking at!" The Point is firmly rooted as Gesture Number One, perhaps because we responded so well to this game.

The Point, she slowly found out, not only brings attention, it can actually bring things to her, like the Force in *Star Wars*. She points to a banana, says *"Da!"* and it is brought to her. Hooray! The glee that shines in her eyes is Frankensteinian sometimes.

Michael

November 10
Whoever designed babies didn't give a damn about parents. How else can you account for babies arriving without teeth? Jessica, our eight-month-old roller coaster, was just seeming to reach a plateau of reason when her mouth began aching, driving her and us nuts. At night, often after midnight, her pain increases — another poor design feature. The first tooth is the worst, supposedly, because the babies don't know what's going on.

This tooth is a landmark, a sign that Jessica is leaving babyhood. As hellish as baby care sometimes is, there have been veins of exquisite joy. The tooth's sudden appearance made me realize how quickly the doll is evolving.

Susan

November 20
"A child pushes buttons in us," Mel Roman, a psychologist I interviewed for an article, told me today. As if I didn't know.

Just look at the way I react to Jessica, popping out of sleep when she's sick as if I'd been shot from a cannon.

It was reassuring to hear Roman say that for every family, the move from two to three members is a giant step, and that problems of adjustment are universal. Sometimes I feel I'm the only woman in the world to have a baby. Alone on earth with my mixed feelings of weariness and exhilaration, restlessness and contentment.

I kept nodding my head in agreement as Roman described how a child upsets a couple's equilibrium, spinning them into a strange world of new decisions, new divisions of affection, new ties with their own parents and with other new parents. I've certainly felt a new link to Mom and Dad since I became a parent, and a powerful need to share the experience with new mothers like Joan.

Along with the new feelings, Roman says a child reintroduces a lot of memories and old conflicts. He braced me for some of the jolts to come when he warned that every aspect of child-raising — weaning, discipline, toilet training — is related to our own experiences. In other words, Michael and I will be dredging up the muck of our own childhoods each step of the way, with Jessica. If Roman is right, we'd better start pulling on our boots.

Michael

November 21
The birth of a child brings more than one new person into the household. Kin from both families move in, via the telephone line. On weekends, when the telephone rates go down, the calls from relatives go up. Much as I like giving hourly activity reports on Jess, I look forward to the day when she can handle her own calls on the hot line.

Susan

November 22

"What a cute baby! How old?" asked the woman by the cigarette machine in the movie theater lobby, not realizing that Jessica's screams had driven me there, and that I was trying to watch the Woody Allen movie through a crack in the door.

Resignedly, I closed the door on Woody, and answered the woman's questions. Later, Michael filled me in on the movie's ending.

Jess used to be as easy as a bag of popcorn to take to the movies, but I guess those days are gone forever. She's no longer content to nurse and nap in the darkened theater, leaving us in peace to watch the screen.

Our blanket policy of taking her everywhere with us is unraveling fast.

Michael

November 28

"What do you want to write about?" said Howard, asking a question that always makes me want to leave the room. It is assumed that writers are born with the zeal to write about a particular topic. I, myself, sometimes confound myself with this damnable question.

Since I know Howard is not being idly curious, nor is he one of those people who simply try to pin you down to put you down, I answered to the best of my ability: I dunno.

Howard, puzzled, asked: "What do you enjoy writing now?" I studied his macrame owl, Danish modern couch and mother-in-law plant, looking for something to prompt an answer. They teleprompted nothing.

Since Jessica's birth, the stories I've felt closest to have been about family issues. But I don't know if they are going to be a long-term inspiration.

Howard suggested that I don't trust my own instincts. That if I enjoy writing about the psychological aspects of family life, I should continue and see where it leads, instead of (as is my habit) undervaluing current pursuits and looking to the future for some incredible fulfillment. Future plans, based on the belief that "I ought to do this," or "I ought to do that," are more likely to lead nowhere, he said. Such abstract goals, he added, tend to become burdensome chores, easily put off. (Don't I know it.)

Do what you want to do, what you feel like doing, not what you think you ought to do, and your chances of happiness and success are a lot better, Howard said.

To have an old problem resolved with common sense in fifty minutes was, of course, humiliating. Jessica, where were you ten years ago?

Michael

November 30
My mother has opened some sort of primal communication with Jessica. During our Thanksgiving weekend in Boston, she spent hours making a continuous half laugh, half jungle-bird sound for Jess. And Jessica responded in kind, stringing together a chain of giggles and chortles. Immediate rapport. For the whole weekend these two wild things whooped it up over nothing.

Jessica's striving for independence took another step forward during our Thanksgiving dinner, when she refused to touch anything that had been cut up into bite-size pieces. No, she wanted whole things. Like a huge drumstick, which she chewed on like a cave baby.

Michael

December 1

Robert Benchley said there are only two ways to travel: first class or with children.

First class with children would be okay. We could use a couple of footmen to carry around the trunks for Jessica's bottles, ointments and diapers (six a day), her wardrobe (she uses up all her clothes in forty-eight hours) and her many appliances. Should servants not be in our immediate future, I must remember a few things:

- Fast starts are a thing of the past. To rush is to end up stuttering like a madman and tripping over tugboats.
- We must allow ourselves a night's sleep between a week of work and a weekend of travel. Last weekend, that might have prevented my driving off with the road atlas still on the car's roof or my making a wrong turn, in my own neighborhood, and getting stuck in a traffic jam for a half hour.
- We must not rent "vehicles" from Rent A Wreck. Avis is damn near as cheap, and their cars have radios, conventional brakes and padded seats, all of which help in traffic jams.

Susan

December 2
Jessica shuddered today when I picked her up. Her back had been turned, and I'd forgotten to warn her I was there with a touch or a word.

Her reaction flashed me back to another child, another scare. I see myself in a yellow sundress that matches my hair, at the zoo with my father. He lifts me up for a better view of the polar bear, a rusty-looking creature with claws like scimitars. From my father's arms I dangle in midair, poised above a pool of alligator-green water that swirls around the bear's rocky den. A chill goes up my bare legs and I scream, "Let me down, Daddy!"

"I won't drop you, I won't drop you," he assures me again and again, but I insist that I can see the bear better through the dirty glass partition. If the bear wants to get me, I feel certain that not even my father can keep me from those curved claws and jagged teeth.

I wonder what Jess feared today, when she suddenly felt my arms locking around her. I hated to see her so shaken and vulnerable, and hated myself for causing her fear. Afterward, we sat in the rocker and I held her close for a while, to reassure us both.

Michael

December 5
Jessica can breathe easy about one thing. She will not automatically inherit the manic-depressive feelings I have toward my mother.

Howard said that the problems a man has with his mother usually crop up in his relationship with his wife, not with his daughter. (Poor Susie!)

Similarly, a man's problems with his father may be reenacted with a son, but rarely with a daughter.

Since my relationship with my father does not seem, at this writing, terribly charged with contradictory emotions, any son I have can also rest easy on this score. (Of course, these words may live to haunt me.)

Michael

December 8

Everybody wants Jessica under their tree for Christmas.

Susie's parents are pushing for a reunion in Key West; mine want us in Boston. Both sets have done everything but write to their congressmen to capture us. "I don't know how many more Christmases we'll both be around," the Cat says, dragging out the death certificates, already frayed and dog-eared from past displays. Susie's mother writes, it seems daily. Gaily asking about our plans.

There is a chance we will end up in Boston by default. We can't really afford the trip to Key West, where Paula and Dennis moved recently. We've looked through all our coat pockets and can't find an extra eight hundred dollars. We could put it on a credit card, but we are already pinched by the monthly debits. Jerome offered to pay for it, but he and Eleanore have already lent us thousands to buy our apartment.

It is a bind.

I feel unusually pulled apart by this simple problem. I guess I feel obliged to share Jessica with the grandparents as much as possible. We want her to have doting grandparents, and we want them to know Jess.

But I wish they would ease off. Parental love can be claustrophobic. Will Susie and I be any different? If not, Jessica, you can throw this diary at us.

Susan

December 10

Michael took Jessica for a stroll along the river tonight, while I finished a phone interview with Loretta Swit, who plays "Hot Lips" on TV's "M*A*S*H." It feels so good to switch roles like this, especially knowing that Michael is as open to the idea as I am.

Loretta talked about the pleasure of being a "M*A*S*H" regular, doing a "beautiful little play every week. There is just no chance to be bored," she said. She also sounded wonderfully comfortable with success. "When opportunities presented themselves I was ready," she said, "and when success came, it was embraceable. I felt I deserved it."

After I hung up the phone, I wished that I'd asked her more questions about living alone, and why she's turned her back on marriage and motherhood. It must take a lot of strength to make that choice. Most of the rest of us tell ourselves we can have it all — marriage, motherhood, career — and then twist ourselves into knots trying to put it all together. Many of my own knots are smoothing out these days, but I think I understand why Loretta, who prizes her career and independence very highly, sticks to the single track.

When Michael returned with Jessica, she seemed cranky about my absence, and ready for a cuddle in the rocker. So, faster than you can say "Loretta Swit," I put aside my pen and rocked, rocked, rocked.

Michael

December 11

"I don't know what's wrong with her tonight," Susie said, as Jessica played out her nightly dinnertime tantrum. When it comes to Jessica, Susie has little memory of yesterday. I wish my memory weren't so long.

The question is: do we (1) continue letting her destroy our dinners, (2) put her to bed when she acts up or (3) postpone our dinner until after she's finally gone to bed? None are appetizing. We muddle along, doing different things different nights.

Michael

December 20

Just one year ago we bought a white sofa. That's how much we knew about children.

Michael / On the Plane from Boston to Key West

December 26

Of all the nutty things. The cheapest tickets to Key West were for a flight originating in Boston the day after Christmas. Susie was weak at the thought of carrying our circus — we are traveling with the usual colossal mound of baggage — on and off planes from New York to Boston, from Boston to Key West and back to New York.

We had a very good time in Boston. When the Cat greeted us, she was wearing a policeman's shirt. It had arm patches depicting a German shepherd with bloody fangs under the words K-9 PATROL. The shirt? "Oh, it turned up in my closet," she said vaguely. Presumably, no body came with it.

All in all, it was about as normal a holiday as could be expected at the Loony Bin (that's the return address on the Cat's stationery). This year's Christmas turkey escaped immolation — in fact, escaped cooking — because of a faulty thermostat and poor quality control (us). After sitting in the slightly warm oven all day, the raw turkey emerged with its white stripes of bacon intact. Emergency rations of meat, purported to be beef, were thawed and grilled on another stove.

Jessica got lots of presents — her favorite was a bag of Susan B. Anthony silver dollars from Grandma Cat — but she also had endless fun playing with the piles of wrapping paper.

Jessica's presence really did charm the occasion. Although she is too young for tales of Santa Claus or stockings on the fireplace mantel, she reminded us all of those days. She was our Christmas angel.

Now, we've left the land of Yule logs and are flying pell-mell to the island of piña coladas and palm trees.

Susan / Key West, Florida

December 28
Christmas in Key West. It sounds good, and feels even better. Raspberry sunsets, pineapple shirts, conch fritters at sidewalk cafés.

We debated until nearly the last minute. Could we afford it? Would we wear ourselves out, traveling with Jessica and all her gear? Finally, family sentiment won out over the ease of staying put.

It was worth it, to see Jess munching papayas in my sister's garden, and sifting sand on my mother's lap at the beach. Surrounded by admirers, Jess has become a shameless flirt, pulling my brother Greg's beard and then disarming him with a twinkly smile.

As Jess skims around Paula's new house in the walker, I'm amazed at her growing mobility. Pumping with her toes, she scuttles sideways like the most agile shellfish, staking out new territory as she spins away from me.

I love her spunk and the new signs of independence, but it's also a bit of a shock. There goes my baby.

Michael

January 1

We brought in the New Year with a yawn, from our bed. Barely awake when the clock struck twelve and eight million other New Yorkers vented pent-up craziness.

It wasn't Jessica's fault, although baby-sitters for New Year's Eve are harder to find than gold. In Miami, our scheduled flight to La Guardia was canceled; when we finally arrived in New York, our mountain of baggage was missing. Two hours later I found the baggage at Kennedy International, but in the meantime lost Susie and Jessica. Dashing through the Siberian winds in my Key West clothes, calling out their names, I fit right into the out-of-kilter New York scene.

Finally, home. We lit a fire, uncorked a bottle of champagne, and exchanged anniversary gifts — for we were married seven New Year's Eves ago. We toasted ourselves and our good fortune, who was snoring in her crib. Still wearing her hat and overcoat.

Susan

January 1
I was tickled by Michael's anniversary gift, a golden seven dangling from a chain. It's been a slightly itchy year for us, but still, a year worth gilding.

Susan

January 3
We're back in the land of mittens and leggings and lap blankets. Brrrrrr.

This morning, getting Jess ready for the baby-sitter, I felt as if I were competing in a decathlon. Could I fill her milk bottle, mix her yogurt and applesauce, stuff her diaper bag, cheer her grumpiness, mop up her breakfast mess, and wrestle her into her snowsuit, all in sixty minutes flat?

On some muddleheaded mornings I'll forget to replenish the diaper supply, or go overboard and pack a week's worth of food. But Ann is so nice — she keeps extra dipes on hand to cover for my lapses, and never teases me about the signs of morning madness.

This morning I'm proud to say that I packed the diaper bag with all the right stuff, zipped the snowsuit without the zipper going off the track, and scraped the cereal spatters off table, walls and floor, all before Ann buzzed the doorbell. I'm still waiting for my gold medal.

Susan

January 5
I've decided that the perfect present for Michael's birthday isn't a present at all, but a surprise party. He'd love to see the house all gaudy with streamers, and jumping with merrymakers. So I've been phoning friends, smuggling bottles of rum into dresser drawers, and stashing party food in the freezer, where Michael never looks. All the work will be worth it, if he's really surprised.

Michael

January 11
Susie's a devil in disguise. Pretending all week that she didn't give a fig about my birthday, then throwing a surprise party for me. It was too much. I almost dropped Jessica when I walked in the door and was greeted by twenty-five friends shouting, *"Surprise!"*

Jessica, however, acted like this kind of thing happens every day.

Susan

January 17

Where are you going?
How late will you be?
Are the windows locked?
How much milk should I give Jessica?
When should I put her to bed?

My head reeled at all the baby-sitter's questions last night. Michael had already escaped out the door, leaving me to face the rapid-fire interrogation.

We're just starting to go out at night without Jess, now that she's a big ten months old. But it's hardly comfortable for me yet. As I exit, I feel as if I'm leaving one arm and one leg behind. And even after we hit our destination, I find myself babbling about Jessica to dinner partners, and feeling strangely bereft as I dance with Michael, without Jess sandwiched between us.

Probably we made things too hard on ourselves, waiting so long to use sitters on weekends. What stopped me in the early months was the worry that no sitter would hold Jess as much as she wants holding. Too easily I could visualize her abandoned in her crib, crying, and disdainful of the bottled milk the sitter offered.

But now that Jess seems comfortable with Ann, her daytime sitter, I'm reassured. I know she won't go hungry, since she takes a bottle easily. I no longer worry about her crying, either, since I choose motherly caregivers like Ann, who don't mind coddling a "lap baby."

Still, I feel a little lost when I leave Jess with someone else. Even someone who asks all the right questions.

Michael

January 20
6:40 A.M.: Susie clogs down the hall to put on coffee. Jessica is awakened by the clogging.

6:41: Michael goes to Jessica's crib. She is standing up, leaning against the rail, vigorously scrubbing her eyes with her knuckles.

She has a salty look. Her hair is blown out into a
golden halo, her cheeks are hot pink and her whole head
is soaking wet. Her wake-up crying stopped when she saw
me. She is very happy to be picked up, gives my shoulder
a hug, pats my back, and chortles as we walk across the
bedroom.

6:42: Jessica resumes crying when she sees Susie is not
in the bedroom. Her cries build to a crescendo; she is not
about to be consoled by Da-da-da.

6:46: Jessica, still sobbing, is at the breast.

7:00: Susie and I are in the kitchen, on automatic pilot,
making breakfast. I lay toys on every surface in the living
room, hoping to keep Jessica busy discovering them. Instead, with a sweep of her arm, she knocks the Activity
Center, toy telephone, musical bears, to the floor.

She turns, her lower lip protruding mischievously, to
get our reaction. "You funny bunny!" Susie says. Jessica
is most pleased. Until she notices that we have put the
gate up at the kitchen entrance. Sensing an abridgment of
civil liberties, she crawls to the gate and shakes it, demanding its removal. Instead, I offer her a box of paper
cups.

Now that's new and interesting.

She spends five entire minutes — an eternity of time for
us — tearing the cups out of the box, fitting them together, and trying to cram the cups back into the box.

7:15: Breakfast is served. Jessica refuses to eat her cereal, will not even touch it. Yesterday, it was her favorite
food. Today, it is viewed with suspicion. I try to put a dab
of it on her lips, so she can reconsider. The cereal lands
on her nose.

7:20: Jessica prefers our bagels and cream cheese. Her
first bite inaugurates her new shock routine. It starts with
a simultaneous sucking in of stomach, expansion of chest

and lowering of chin. (Try it.) In this position, she furrows her brow and attempts to look horrified, but a suppressed smile gets the better of her. The shock routine ends with her shaking her head sideways and rearing backward. What a monkey.

7:30: Jessica is done. Tosses the remainder of her bagel on the floor. Now she *wants*. We try water, milk, more bagel. No good. She begins pointing. The knife? No, you can't have that. She seems to want out of her seat; I lift her to the floor. She cries, as though she's been rejected. I pick her up and bring *Milton the Early Riser* over to the sofa to read to her. Nope, she worms out of my lap.

7:40: Jessica crawls over to Susie, attaches herself to the breast with a deep, deep sigh.

Michael

January 23
Susie called up every teenager in Brooklyn but couldn't find one to sit for Jess Saturday night. So we took her with us to Carolyn's party. Why not? Baby goes everywhere, right? (That is, except to those museums, restaurants and theaters that ban dogs and midgets.)

Everything was fine until about ten o'clock. I had danced around with Jessica laughing on my hip, and everybody said we were the best-looking couple on the floor. Then Jessica began to crash, and was unusually upset. The noise, excitement and smoke at the party must have gotten to her. Susie nursed her to sleep and put her on Carolyn's bed, which had a pile of the guests' winter coats on one side.

About a half hour later, one of the guests was a bit freaked when she heard a baby's cries coming from the bedroom but couldn't see a baby. She told Carolyn and Susie, who rushed in and found a pile of winter coats on top of Jessica. She was okay, just shaken up by the breathless darkness.

Apparently, somebody had either mistaken Jess for a blond fur or hadn't seen her; at any rate, one coat led to another until a pile developed on top of her.

In retrospect, it wasn't smart of us to rest her there on the bed, even though that appeared to be the quietest, safest place in the apartment. Veteran parents, I'm sure, would have surveyed the scene and gone home, no matter how much they were enjoying themselves. Carolyn's party was our rite of passage.

Susan

January 26
Pins, pennies, paper clips terrify me, now that Jessica crawls everywhere.

Yesterday, Michael saw Jess pick up a penny that had rolled under the radiator. He bolted toward her. She gulped and licked her lips.

First Michael turned her upside down, hoping that if she had swallowed the penny, it would dislodge. Nothing. Then we searched her clothes, the floor, the furniture. Still no penny.

At such moments, I become a crazy person, while Michael seems able to reach back for some stored wisdom that saves the day. In this case, he recalled reading somewhere that as long as an object doesn't lodge on the way down, it will show up in the diaper with no harm done.

But now we think that Jess didn't swallow it after all,

because no penny has turned up in the diaper. Meanwhile, our little piggy bank remains in perfect health.

I hope she doesn't try to beat the record of her Boston friend, Will, who has bolted down about twenty cents in small change.

Michael

January 28
As I pulled off her blue overalls, Jessica knew it was Tub Time, our nightly ritual. "Okay! All right!" she as much as said with her squeals of delight.

Naked as the days we were born, we jump into the deep, causing a traffic jam of tugboats, barges, ducks, a rubber hammer, empty shampoo bottles and plastic boxes. For the next twenty minutes Jessica forgets I exist. I am a place to sit and a thing that recirculates toys. She concentrates on the business at hand: figuring out what this water stuff is and how these colored things move on it.

A stream of high-pitched nonsense syllables accompanies the sinking of ships, the squeezing of ducks and the chewing of sea captains. Never still for a second, she clambers over me to grab a floating rattle, loses her footing, slips partially under the water and comes up gasping, as though she has seen the Loch Ness monster down there.

Then, when the toys seem to offer no new amusement and she has tired of fiddling with the faucets, she discovers me. "Oy day, oy day," she says, looking me over, assessing my toy potential. A couple of pinches, she figures, is all I am worth. "Ouch! Ouchee!" I say, and she giggles and pinches again. Jessica knows pain, she has bumped her head a few times, but she does not understand the mechanics of it. It's fine for her to pinch me, but when I pinch her, she looks at me as though I'm Vincent Price.

She pulls herself up, her waist level with the tub rim and her belly arcing out in front of her. I poke it. She buckles her eyebrows in a frown and tosses me an oblique look. What an actress. Then, ever so casually, she experiments with this belly thing. She tries to pull her stomach in, and starts to contract the right muscles, but loses interest as her eyes fasten on the bar of Ivory Soap floating by. She loves Ivory, could spend hours chasing it all over the tub.

"No, honey, it is not good to eat," I say. Jessica, however, believes I am just trying to spoil the fun. She struggles the soap away from me, taunts me by pretending to put it in her mouth. "It's pewy," I tell her, each time it nears her mouth. Interest in the game fades and she takes a bite of Ivory and instantly cries, giving me a blameful, tearful look, as though she were saying, "Why didn't you tell me?"

She pulls my palm to her mouth and starts drinking, even though there is no water there. She is so used to my cupping a hand under the faucet to give her a drink, she thinks I've got magic palms with springs in them. You can't get more innocent than that.

Susan

January 30
"What I need," I've been telling Michael, "is a giant rubber mallet that wouldn't hurt Jess, just stun her into submission."

He laughed and agreed as we both dashed after our little blond housewrecker, who can rearrange any room in ten seconds flat.

Michael

January 30
Feeling like an extraordinarily well-integrated person now. For the first time in memory, I feel emotionally clean. My head is clear. No loose anxieties rattling around, making a mess of everything. They are now reattached to their original problems and the problems are relatively straightforward.

Howard, however, chided me today for "acting as though I were a very simple person." He apparently knows something I don't, but I like feeling simple.

Michael

January 31
As I look back through the pages of this diary, it seems as though I have written a great deal about troubled feelings, less about the pleasures of being a father. One reason for this is that problems motivate me to write sense into them, but good times don't have to make sense, and may go unreported.

In many ways, this has been a very sober year for me. The rewards, I sense, are just beginning to topple in. Susie is more relaxed and enthusiastic now that her writing fits well with her new life. Jessica is becoming more responsive, and, most of the time, has the same effect on me as the Swiss Alps. She's a challenge, but an exhilarating one.

Michael

February 2
Jessica is a toy junkie.

She has to have a curious object, preferably in each hand, at all times. Or else delirium sets in. She insatiably devours experience, wrings newness out of every object and discards it. Most objects yield their secrets quickly, in a matter of seconds, and require instant replacement.

So far, store-bought toys give the briefest, least substantial yield, and, as far as I can see, aren't worth buying at all. Jess can squeeze the juice out of a $2.95 duck in a flash, never to return to it with more than a jaded interest. But the bright box that the duck came in, now that's an endless source of pleasure. She can manipulate the box, squeeze it, tear it, open it, close it, eat it, sit on it. But she can't interact as much with the duck, so that sits in the tub, waiting to occupy a single moment of the next tub time.

Great toys are wooden spoons and bowls, contact-lens cases and small objects of any sort. Ball-point pens, unfortunately, rank high on her list. I am afraid she will stick one in her eye, but it is impossible to keep her hands off them. Crayons, to her, don't make it.

Books are now her favorite pastime. She is wild about picture books with cats and dogs and children. She points at the pictures, slaps the pages, and bucks her bottom in excitement. She has a very discerning eye for illustration, too. She doesn't like the goofy drawings found in many

213

children's books, and won't tolerate fake colors or too much detail. Strange then, isn't it, that good picture books are hard to find, yet the toy stores are packed with plastic crap that interests her not a whit.

Susan

February 11
Jessica scratched my cornea when she poked me in the eye last week, and I'm just now getting back to normal.

It happened at a Mass in honor of my grandfather's ninetieth birthday. We had rented a car and gone back to the coal region for the family reunion my mother had arranged. Car trips always spin Jessica to sleep, so she was an angel for the first half of the service. But by Communion time she had turned devilish again, bobbing around the pew, itchy for action. When she poked me, I didn't blink in time. A visit to the eye doctor confirmed the scratch, and he gave me some ointments to ease the broken-glass sensation. For days afterward I reached for those little tubes like a drug addict, desperate for the soothing creams.

I snapped at Michael the morning after we got back, when he brought Jessica to me for her usual nursing. "I can't even see her. How am I going to do it?" I demanded crossly. Calmly and silently he got us all arranged and then disappeared to make coffee.

Sitting there in bed, unable to open the sore eye and with Jessica on top of me, I felt the weight of motherhood more than I ever have before. In sickness and in health, till death do us part. . . .

Michael

February 12

There is no sick leave from motherhood. When Susie was abed this past week, all was chaos.

The apartment, which magically remains neat in normal times, began to grow heaps of clothing on every surface. Stacks of newspapers and dishes leapt onto tables. Baggage from the Pennsylvania trip lay about the walkways, torn open and pillaged for essentials.

The crunch came Monday morning. Susie was in bed, stiffly motionless, stoically bearing the pain and breast-feeding Jessica. Jess drank merrily, pointed at her mother's inflamed eye, and made her usual exclamatory sounds.

When she finished her milk, I put Jess in the aluminum walker, which she promptly capsized. She landed with a thump, facedown on the hardwood floor. Shock held her cries for a moment, then they burst loose. Blood was dripping from her mouth.

"Damn it! I think she broke her only tooth," I said, as I lowered the bawling babe onto Susie's breast. "Her only tooth!" Susie said. "Why does everything go wrong at once?"

When Jessica finally calmed down and we were able to wash away the blood, her Chiclet of a tooth was still there! Jessica had only bitten her upper lip.

In retrospect, it would have made great sense for me to take time off work during Susie's recovery. But I never thought of it. I am still running on my old schedule of priorities, where work automatically takes precedence. Not so from now on.

Susan

February 14
At the home of friends tonight, Jess suddenly lurched from her upright position at the coffee table's edge, to the couch where I was sitting. A distance of one giant step, or so it must have seemed to Jess while she was in full tilt. Her eyes were saucers of amazement when she landed safely against my legs. As if she'd just walked on the moon.

"Michael, did you see that?" I cried.

Thrilled with her courage, we rewarded our moon-walker with pats, kisses and praise. Never mind that this is the beginning of lots of new trouble.

Our friends, childless and only mildly impressed, couldn't begin to understand what all the excitement was about.

Michael

February 16
Jessica climbs into her cane rocking chair, grabs a book, and starts reading *Milton the Early Riser*. "Dee! Da!" she says, pointing at pictures of Milton the baby panda dancing in his bamboo jungle. Flip, flip, flip, the book is absorbed, tossed on the floor, and replaced by *I Can Count to 100 — Can You?* And so it goes: on to the Next Thing, and the Next Thing and the Next. A curiosity that knows one boundary: sleep.

This child has an omnivorous, insatiable mind. I get tired just watching her. Every single minute, she's learning something new. No adult could possibly keep up with a child's intellectual curiosity. Sometimes, as I pass her books, toys, hats, rings and anything else handy, I wonder how the Einsteins coped with little Albert.

Susan

February 17
Now that Jess is on her way to toddlerhood, I'm warming up my interest in older children. "Does your daughter play on her own very much now?" I asked the mother of a four-year-old, when we met at the playground.

"Not really," was her disappointing answer. "Her favorite game is pretending. She'll say, 'Pretend I'm a tiger and you're the circus lady.'"

All mothers have to be circus ladies, I've decided, to keep up with their kids.

Michael

February 18
As we picked a path through the filth and human debris in Times Square last night, en route to the other world of ballet, I thought, "I don't want Jessica to grow up here."

I don't want to grow up here, either, now that I think about it.

We came to New York because it is the most exciting place in the world and because it offers unbelievable career opportunities. It's the front line for most professions and, like any battle zone, it has casualties and constantly needs new recruits.

We came with a Five Year Plan that called for us to build up our résumés and portfolios and then take them to the city of our choice, possibly San Francisco or Boston.

This is the Fifth Year. But New York has seduced us, hooked us, and weakened our wills to leave. We've got good friends here, good jobs, and we're just beginning to have the time and money needed to enjoy the city's vast resources. We no longer say we're passing through: it's home.

Enter Jessica.

New York is suddenly put in a new perspective, the one I had on first arrival, when I put my money in my shoes to foil muggers. It took me a few years to acquire a taste for this teeming island of concrete, and I think it might take a child far longer.

As I carry her interests with me now, as a measure of all things, I realized that "Jessica" is actually an excuse for my deepest, truest feelings. She has ripped a jaded veneer off life, and I am looking at everything with fresh eyes. She is my magic charm.

Susan

February 19

Break out the wineglasses. Tonight I put Jessica into her crib at nine o'clock, without a lot of endless rocking and nursing, and she pressed her cheek into the mattress and obligingly went to sleep. Just the way it's supposed to happen.

Could I have done the same thing weeks ago? Months ago? Who knows the answers to these perplexing questions.

By comforting Jessica each time she cried, I've tried to ease her entrance into this cruel world. If rocking her to sleep each night has been a mistake, so be it. There will be plenty of others.

Michael

February 19
Jessica loved pulling records off the shelf and out of their jackets. Then she threw them around or tried to eat them, doing the devil's work on the plastic grooves. In five minutes, fifty records rolled. Up until now, those five minutes of her preoccupation were worth more to us than the collected works of Mozart and the Rolling Stones combined.

But, in a fleeting moment of clarity, I taped up the records so securely that none of us can play with them. Now, why didn't I think of that before? Well, I think I am getting a second wind of fatherhood. I am coming to grips with the realities of family life. Some things, like our record collection, are temporarily out of service, and I am finding it's best to make the adjustment as swiftly and cleanly as possible.

Susan

February 20
"Hello, mousie," croons my distant cousin, a Fifth Avenue mother of five older children, when first she sees Jessica. A moment before, she was talking about tennis and a trip to Puerto Rico. Now she forgets everything else and sings to Jessica in a little-girl warble: "The babies on the bus go wah-wah-wah, / Wah-wah-wah, / Wah-wah-wah, / The babies on the bus . . ."

Amused, I watch her transformation from worldly matron to baby-crazy mother. How easily these twists of sweet cream, these babies, set our senses reeling. What delicious, dangerous power they have over us.

It makes me think of the other night, when Michael and I watched the newborn daughter of some friends so that they could have dinner in town. I was amazed at how I melted when the baby's fuzzy head nuzzled my neck. Baby-weary though I sometimes feel, that old baby magic still works on me, too.

Michael

February 23
Why was having a baby such a shock? Why did it put me into a numbed state, from which it took months to recover?

Two answers landed on my desk at work: *Between Generations: The Six Stages of Parenthood* by Ellen Galinsky, and *Ourselves and Our Children* by the Boston Women's Health Book Collective. My interests and the Style Page's overlapped, so I had the pleasure of interviewing the authors.

"Being a parent is supposed to be second nature, like eating and sleeping," said Peggy Wegman, a Boston therapist and one of the authors of *Ourselves and Our Children.* "People have been taken in by this myth," she continued. "They are not prepared for a real identity crisis, a total reorganization of their lives, because it's very difficult to see something that isn't culturally accepted. In our culture, we value profit, progress, efficiency — parenting is anything but those things."

Cultural conditioning, she added, allows parents to share their "glories and war stories," but keeps them from talking about their deeper feelings. In *Ourselves and Our Children,* one hundred couples share their disappointments over such things as a child's appearance, a grandparent's reaction to a child, anxiety about the loss of a sexual relationship with a spouse.

I wish I had seen this book a year ago.

Ellen Galinsky, author of the *Stages* books, said that fantasies, many of them culturally conditioned, play a major role in determining people's reactions to parenthood. People create images of future events, she said, and are happy when the event conforms to the image. But when reality and the image are incongruous, parents may be angry and depressed, consciously or unconsciously.

I now see that I was angry and depressed, on probably all psychic levels, when the teeth-cracking reality of coping with infant Jessica violated my misty notions of familial bliss. Ah, those early days of incongruity.

In her book, Ellen identifies six stages, between pregnancy and the time a child leaves home, when parents confront their images and either resolve the conflicts and grow, or develop problems.

"Positive growth occurs when an image is modified to be consistent with reality or when behavior is modified to reach toward an image," Ellen wrote.

As Howard would say, it resonates.

Well, Jess, one stage down and five to go. At least we've got a one-year breather before tackling your next stage, the legendary Terrible Twos. Though I may be in for another painful growth spurt, I imagine that the most stunning pains are the first ones.

Susan

February 24
From our window I see past shops, trees and rooftops into another apartment window: a new mother, nursing her

baby. One look, and I'm back to my own early days with Jess.

I'd like to send that other mother some flowers, tell her all I know about the mercurial early months. One morning, your baby is a little egg with apricot feathers for hair. Another morning, you wake up to a pink and perfect person, who's laughing and yowling and threatening to yank herself out of your arms.

I feel like telling that new mother that she's doing the right thing, nursing and rocking and hugging her baby while the rest of the world zooms by. I realize now that those close, sometimes claustrophobic days are over too soon. It's hard living through them, harder still to let them go.

Michael

February 25
From skin to snowsuit is an incredible distance.

First the diapers. Jessica does not like diapers. Invariably, it is a wild, bare-bottom scramble over the bed. (We skimped, didn't buy a changing table. So for months we've slept with A & D ointment, occasionally a diaper pin or damp spot.) After the initial frenzy of the diaper chase, Jessica passively accepts her waterproof pants — so long as she has a toy in hand. The box of baby wipes will do. Here the game is to sneak one into her mouth while I'm busy. She never believes me when I tell her lanolin is not good to eat.

Undershirt? Okay, she'll cooperate with that. Shirt? Nope, the squirm begins anew. Corduroy pants? *She's had it.* "Lemme go, you brute," her cries imply. A new cry is miraculously created. It has a warble like a police siren, caused by big dramatic sobs as she inhales and exhales. We both get a kick out of it. Momentarily, it distracts her.

Into the living room we go, to find more toys to distract. Absentmindedly, she cooperates with the sweater layer by switching her truck from one hand to the other while each sleeve is pulled on.

Suddenly, she's hot from all the squirming and layers of clothes. Plucking madly at her sweater buttons, wailing at the sight of her leggings going on. She is incredulous. Her theatrical look says: "More clothes? You've *got* to be kidding! I'm already broiling."

Finally, the last round of heavy socks, overcoat, hat and mittens. In trying to tug her hat off, she pulls it over her face, gets scared, and emits a single strand of sound that makes the eardrums tickle.

Jessica is dressed.

Susan

February 27

"We're thinking about it, too," said the young lawyer we met at a dinner party tonight. "It" is having a baby, and I can see by his giddy smile that he knows no more about the whole process than we did. But that doesn't stop him from rushing in where angels fear to tread.

"We've debated it back and forth," he tells us. "My wife is thirty-three, time is running out . . ." His eyes are spinning with baby daydreams as he poses the cosmic question, "What else is there in life, anyway?" Clearly, he's a goner.

Michael and I listen sympathetically, nodding in unison. We could give some cautionary advice, curb his mounting enthusiasm, but of course we don't. When hormones are careening and visions of babies dancing, a couple is not going to make an intellectual decision about having a child. They are going to do what we did: jump in feetfirst.

Michael

February 27
I have known it for a few weeks now, but hearing it from Howard made me feel good: I can end the therapy sessions anytime now. My questions were answered, by me as well as by Howard.

I am going to continue for a while, just to make sure everything has been ironed out. (Howard says I am adept at repressing unpleasantries, until they ultimately repress me.) It is remarkable that thirty-four years of confusion has been cleared up in only a few months.

I can't believe the depth of my good feelings for myself.

Susan

March 2
To the shoe store for Jessica's first pair. We chose the smallest sneakers made, in navy blue with snubby rubber toes. It hurts my sense of fairness that a few inches of canvas cost fifteen dollars.

The salesman tried to talk me into some white high-tops, too, but I couldn't be persuaded. Dr. Finkelman says to go with the high-tops only if they're a gift from Grandma.

In the new shoes Jess clumped around the store like Baby Frankenstein, clinging to the carpeted platforms and poking one foot woodenly in front of the other. I watched her with a mixture of delight and dread. My "lap baby" will be running laps before I know it.

As I rolled Jess out of the store in her stroller, I could tell she was pleased with her new shoes, because she smiled down at her feet and tapped both heels together.

Susan

March 5

The experts say you should never let your bedroom be the place where you also do your work. Making love and making money aren't supposed to mix.

But what else can I do? Now that Jess is nearly a year old, she needs her own room. That means giving up the little den that has served as my office, and making part of our bedroom my workplace.

I loved the sunny little den, with its view of Victorian cupolas and flowering window boxes. I dread dismantling my files and relocating my desk. But Michael is insistent. He says we need to reclaim our privacy as a couple by sleeping alone.

He's right, of course, but I'm less rational on the subject. The office has been a symbol of my life apart from him and Jess, and it's hard to let go of that feeling of separateness. In fact, whenever I think of giving up the office, I go into mourning.

But I guess I'd better take down the black crepe and get out the dustcloths. Jess's new room must shine for her birthday. I've got some soft white curtains, a ruffly pastel quilt to hang above her crib. I'm glad she'll have a pretty new place of her own.

Still, it's sobering to realize that there will be lots of other compromises to come; that I'll probably spend the rest of my life sorting out what I owe to Michael, to Jessica, and to myself.

Susan

March 7
The new office isn't so bad, after all. Michael did a beautiful job of organizing the space for me, with a built-in desk, vertical files, bookshelves. On the wall he hung favorite photos of Jess at the beach, my mother as a baby-faced college girl. I like the pictures because they warm up the brick wall and give me a peaceful feeling as I work. It warms me, too, that Michael tried so hard to make the new office as good as it could be.

Michael

March 7
How do people do it? After having one child, you would think they would know better than to have another. Not that I regret having Jessica; quite the contrary. But why two? Isn't that greedy? As well as exhausting?

Susie and I often discuss whether to have Number Two. We adore Jess, and we are sure we would adore her bookend. The idea of another baby appeals to me in the abstract but I wonder if we've got the energy to commit ourselves to another child. A second child would mean more sacrifice, just at the time when we're beginning to enjoy a respite. It would mean putting off Susie's and my reunion as a couple for another block of time.

But who knows?

Practically speaking, Number Two would be infinitely easier to accommodate than Number One. Jessica has already plowed the field, dug out the tree stumps and rocks. Our emotions are now, more or less, in orderly rows and our life-style is geared to hers. The adaptation process for another child wouldn't be nearly so great.

All indications point to making such a decision. Having one child sets up a momentum and, to stop it, there has to be a conscious decision not to have more. Do we want an "only child"? Will Jess mind being the only minor in the family? Wouldn't it be healthier for Jess if there were another child to share the spotlight of parental hopes and fears? Wouldn't it be better for her to learn sharing at home?

On the flip side, as a single child, Jess will be the sole beneficiary of our limited measures of time and money. Would we really have the resources to raise two children? A year ago I didn't know if I could handle one child.

And would Jessica, in reality, resent her sibling? Or vice versa? As the youngest in my own family, I know that having older brothers means having playmates, but it also means having playmates who are always better at everything — and not shy about saying so.

We are going to wait until Jessica is two and a half before seriously considering it. Then we will know a little more about Jessica and ourselves. In the final analysis, Susie will be the one casting the deciding ballot. She's the one who makes these babies and it's her career that would be most dislocated.

The second-child decision is almost no different from the first-child decision. Not easy.

Susan

March 8
Sleeping without Jessica in our room does make a difference. When the lights go out, Michael and I are back to
where we started.

Susan

March 9
We lit one pink candle for Jessica today. I filled the punch
bowl, Jess put on her best pinafore, Michael took home
movies of my parents and a cluster of friends, making
faces and crooning the birthday song. It was a silly, senti-
mental day.

In the middle of all the excitement, the birthday girl
calmly abandoned her guests and gifts to take a nap. Two
hours later, tousle-headed, she slipped back into the mer-
riment, tearing at ribbons and leaving a trail of cake
crumbs everywhere.

While I was alone with Joan for a moment, I whispered
that my period came back today. She agreed that it is
strangely symbolic that one year from the day I bore Jess,
I'm fertile again. The prospect of having another child still
seems distant, but today brought the question into closer
focus. Will there be other babies? I wonder.

For now, it's enough to savor this day, celebrate our
first year as a family. So we lit one pink candle for Jessica,
and there's one for us all to grow on.

Michael

March 12
For the three of us, this has been a year of amazing struggles and amazing growth. Jessica, where are you taking us
now?